Serged Garments
in Minutes

OTHER BOOKS AVAILABLE FROM CHILTON
Robbie Fanning, Series Editor

Serged Garments in Minutes

A Complete Guide to
Simple Construction Techniques

Tammy Young and Naomi Baker

Chilton Book Company
Radnor, Pennsylvania

Acknowledgments

Many popular serger construction techniques have been developed by both industry professionals and serger-sewing enthusiasts before and during the time we were refining and developing ours. We want to thank the one person who has given us the most inspiration and encouragement, our friend Gail Brown. Her inventive mind continues to challenge and stimulate us; and, more specifically, she has originated several of the serger techniques presented here.

We also want to thank two other very hard-working, talented people without whom our books could not be completed. Chris Hansen is our incomparable illustrator, a sewing and serging whiz, and our good friend. He not only beautifully illustrates what we are trying to describe, but he catches our boo-boos, too. And many thanks to Cate Keller Lowe who has been involved in our books since the beginning. Now she not only watches

unerringly over all the last-minute details, but has provided her design and layout talents as well.

Finally, many thanks go to our series editor, Robbie Fanning, and to the entire Chilton team for their support, encouragement, and professionalism.

The following are registered trademark names used in this book: *Lycra, Organ, Pattern Pals, Seams Great, Stitch 'n Stretch, Velcro,* and *Washaway.*

Copyright © 1992 by Tammy Young and Naomi Baker
All Rights Reserved
Published in Radnor, Pennsylvania 19089, by Chilton Book Company
No part of this book may be reproduced, transmitted or stored in any form or by any means,
electronic or mechanical, without prior written permission from the publisher

Designed by Anthony Jacobson
Manufactured in the United States of America

Library of Congress Cataloging in Publication Data
Young, Tammy
    Serged garments in minutes: a complete guide to simple construction techniques/
Tammy Young and Naomi Baker.
       p. cm. — (Creative machine arts series)
    Includes index.
    ISBN 0-8019-8354-1
    1. Serging 2. Clothing and dress. I. Baker, Naomi. II. Title. III. Series
TT713.Y685 1992   92-23595
646.2'044—dc20   CIP

2 3 4 5 6 7 8 9 0   9 8 7 6 5 4 3

Contents

Foreword

I had a hunch I would like *Serged Garments in Minutes* even before I read it. Of all the serger experts in the field, I predicted that Naomi Baker and Tammy Young would handle this in-demand topic uniquely, thoroughly, and creatively.

Well, my hunch was right: without ever lapsing into tedium, this book tells and shows the easiest, fastest, and most professional ways to integrate serged construction into just about any garment. I get countless questions about this very subject—in particular, "Where should I sew, and where should I serge?"—and I'm so glad to finally have a ready title to recommend.

And the timing of this book couldn't be better. When home-use sergers were first being discovered by seamsters, many understandably skipped the obvious—serging to speed, streamline, and improve construction—to play with yummy decorative threads and finishing. Now, it seems, as embellishment trends ebb and flow, enthusiasts are returning to the whys and hows of serged-garment assembly. Luckily they can also return to this book for all the answers.

You'll also discover that "reading" this book often isn't reading at all. It's instantly understanding a technique, or serging order, because of Chris Hansen's friendly, enlightening artwork. You've seen his drawings in my

collaborations with Tammy— *Innovative Sewing* and *Innovative Serging*—in the other Chilton books by both of these talented authors, and the *Update Newsletters*. In addition to his artistic abilities, Chris's passion for sewing and fashion put him in a class by himself. I know you'll enjoy and appreciate his work.

So do as Naomi and Tammy say: "Cut through the talk and serge something!" following their well-researched instructions. Your sewing and serging productivity will increase, and your garment quality will improve—all great reasons to buy, read, and treasure this book.

Gail Brown
Co-author, *Innovative Serging*

Preface

While reading all the conventional sewing-machine techniques on your pattern's instructions, have you ever asked yourself how you can use your serger instead? Then this book is for you!

After many requests, we decided to compile all of our favorite simple and speedy serger garment-construction ideas and applications in one handy reference. In this first-ever book exclusively devoted to the subject, we've included information about where and how to use your serger when constructing any garment.

We recommend that you read *Serged Garments in Minutes* through from cover to cover to learn new serging construction techniques and review old favorites, and then keep the book nearby as a helpful reference when planning any garment-construction project.

As we began organizing this book, we realized that we couldn't include all serger-sewing information, so we sorted out the best and fastest. When we left out techniques, it was because they were less durable or professional-looking or because the ones we included were easier.

During our research, we challenged ourselves to find ways to use the serger on many garment areas which are traditionally sewn with the conventional machine—for example, keyhole openings, plackets, vents, and slits. We also pulled together guidelines on serged seams, ribbing, elastic, and hems and assembled them into helpful

charts throughout the book. Plus we developed several new serged construction techniques such as clean-finished elastic button loops, tulip pockets, double pockets, and a mock tailored placket.

* NOTE: THROUGHOUT, GRAY SHADING IN ALL ILLUSTRATIONS DENOTES THE RIGHT SIDE OF FABRIC.
◯ RIGHT SIDE OF FABRIC
◯ WRONG SIDE OF FABRIC

After carefully analyzing several previously published serging techniques, we made refinements on those as well. For example, you'll find our recommended methods have changed for flatlocking a double hem and serging a slash pocket, a constructed waistband, and a one-step banded waistline casing. We've also added simple instructions for converting traditional sewing applications (such as front-hip pockets, lining, self-welt pockets, and a tucked sleeve finish) to serging.

In garment construction, the sewing machine and serger work in tandem. Although some couture garments do not include serging and some casual sportswear is made by serging alone, most garments can be made

more professionally and efficiently using both machines. In this book, you'll learn where and when to use which for the best results. For a step-by-step guide to adapting several popular garment styles to serger construction, see the eight color pages we've included.

Because new products and techniques are constantly being developed, we couldn't include every possible eventuality in this book. But don't worry; with the fundamentals you will learn here, you can develop new methods, too. When unique construction problems arise, test the options on scraps to discover the best technique before applying to it to your garment.

Although some decorative serging applications are included as part of the garment construction in this book, it is not meant to be a book about decorative serging. For the latest decorative serging and embellishment techniques, as well as numerous easy serger projects, see the *Know Your Serger* series listed in "Other Books by the Authors" on page 136.

We feel confident that this book can save you time and give your serging professional-looking results. We also hope that it will inspire you to develop new serging techniques of your own— please let us know what you discover!

Happy serging,

Tammy Young
Naomi Baker

CHAPTER 1

SPEEDY CONSTRUCTION SECRETS

Speedy Construction Secrets

Cut Through the Talk—Let's Make Something! ✁ Get Ready—Gather the Supplies
Get Set—Review the Basics ✁ Go—Begin with a Simple Pullover Top ✁ Serge Foolproof Pull-on Pants

Cut Through the Talk—Let's Make Something!

Ever feel that way when you decide to learn something new? "Just show me how to do it," you say. "Let me get started." That's exactly what we're going to do in this chapter.

Using a 3- or 4-thread serger, you'll make a basic pullover top and pull-on pants of either knit or woven fabric to see firsthand just how easy serged garment construction can be. In less than one hour of serging time, you'll sew an entire outfit. (Fig. 1-1)

Then you'll go on to learn how to use your serger for all the basics of garment construction, whether or not you are an experienced seamstress (but it does help to know basic sewing-machine skills and sewing techniques). You can use our simple tips and techniques to serge garments quickly and easily.

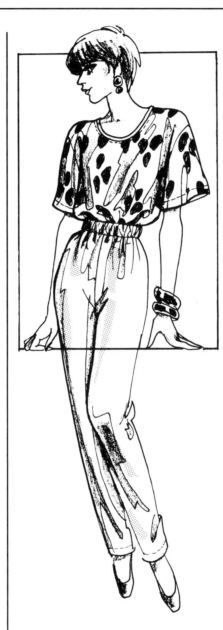

Fig. 1-1 Serge a simple outfit quickly and easily.

When we introduce serger techniques in this clothing construction book, we assume that you know serger basics:

✁ Threading your serger

✁ Changing stitch length and width

✁ Adjusting tension

✁ Using differential feed, if available on your machine

✁ Converting to a rolled edge and a flatlock stitch

✁ Securing seam ends

✁ Removing serged stitching

✁ Serging curves, corners, and angles

✁ Clearing the stitch finger

✁ Serging terminology, for example, definition of stitch types (see Glossary).

If you aren't familiar with these basic serging techniques, *ABCs of Serging,* another book coauthored by Tammy Young, will familiarize you with the fundamentals (see "Other Books by the Authors" in the back of this book). If you need a refresher about terms like **serge-finish** or **balanced stitch**, see the Glossary.

Get Ready—Gather the Supplies

Pullover top pattern—Choose a basic pullover pattern for wovens or knits with short or long sleeves and a round, faced neckline. Be sure the top is designed to be pulled on over the head without an opening. You will finish the neckline with a narrow bias band, so the facing pattern piece will not be used. Make any fitting alterations to the pattern (except at the neckline edge) before cutting. (Fig. 1-2)

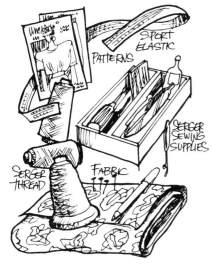

Fig. 1-2 Before beginning, gather the necessary supplies.

Pull-on pants pattern—Select an elastic-waist pattern without a separate waistband, for wovens or knits. A one-piece pattern (without side seams) is faster to sew and the fitting can be done during construction. Purchase the pattern by your hip measurement and make length alterations, if necessary, following the shorten/lengthen lines on the pattern. If you are unsure about your crotch length, add 1" to the upper edge of the pattern piece(s) on both the front and back.

Compare your bust, hip, and finished-length measurements to the measurements on the back of the pattern envelope, and make the necessary alterations. If your pattern does not specify a sleeve or arm length, measure the pattern piece to your arm. For accuracy, you may need to pin the sleeve pattern to the front pattern piece so the shoulder seam will be correctly positioned before measuring the sleeve length. (Fig. 1-3)

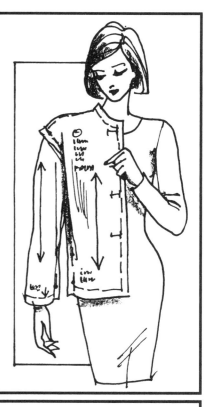

Fig. 1-3 Pin-fit the pattern to check the sleeve length.

Choose a pattern that calls for a wider elastic, such as 1-1/2"-wide sport elastic. It is the most comfortable to wear and the wider width is easier to wear under a belt. If your pattern calls for narrower elastic, extend the fold-over casing on both the front and back of the pattern so that it equals two times the width of the elastic plus 1/4". (Fig. 1-4)

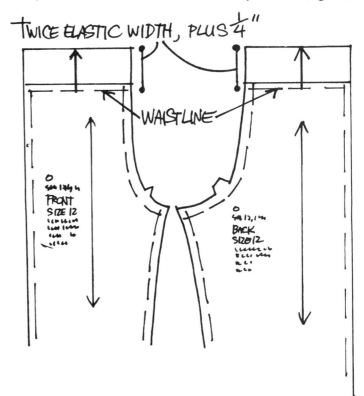

Fig. 1-4 If necessary, adjust the casing for wider elastic.

Fabric—Choose a knit or a tightly woven material such as a rayon, silky, or lightweight cotton sheeting for both the top and the pants. Use matching or coordinating solids or prints.

> **Serged seams are most durable on tightly woven fabric. They will not pull off or ravel away during wear.**

Serger thread—Find three or four spools or cones (depending whether you'll use a 3- or 3/4-thread stitch) to match or coordinate with your fabric.

Sport elastic—You'll need enough 1-1/2"-wide sport elastic to fit comfortably around your waistline. This is a knit elastic that won't stretch out of shape during top-stitching.

Basic serging supplies—Put your serging supplies in a handy carryall or keep them together within easy reach. Don't forget the accessories and attachments included with your machine, tweezers, spare machine needles and a needle inserter or needle-nose pliers, seam sealant, a loop turner or darning needle, disappearing marking pens, and other conventional sewing supplies.

Get Set—Review the Basics

Cutting

Pretreat the fabric with the same care method you will be using after wearing. Cut the top and the pants following the pattern layouts, eliminating the neckline facing. For a neckline band, cut a 1-1/4" by 25" bias strip from woven fabric (or a crossgrain strip on knit fabric). (Piece if necessary.) Save some of the scraps to test your serging.

Pin-basting

We prefer serging without pinning, but if you are using a silky fabric and are more comfortable using pins, take extra care to keep the pins away from the knives. You may pin parallel to the seam to the left of the stitching line. Be careful to remove the pins before they reach the presser foot. (Fig. 1-5) (More information about pinning is featured in Chapter 3.)

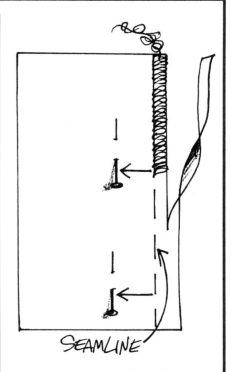

Fig. 1-5 Pin-baste to the left of the seamline if you pin at all.

> **Try finger-pinning to position seamlines for serging. Secure one end of the seamline with the needle and presser foot. Then hold the matching seam layers at the midpoint of the seamline and at the hem. Serge, releasing the finger-pinning when the foot reaches it. (Fig. 1-6)**

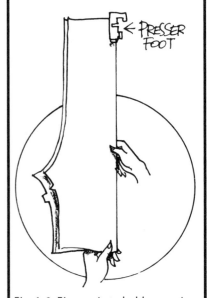

Fig. 1-6 Finger-pin to hold seams in position when serging.

Seaming

Using a 3- or 4-thread serger, adjust for a wide, medium-length, balanced stitch. Serge with the needle (the left needle of a 3/4-thread machine) on the seamline and let the knives trim the extra seam allowance. For a narrower 3-thread stitch, you may want to straight-stitch the seam, then serge-seam the allowances together close to the seamline. Test seaming two layers of scraps together, both on the lengthwise and the crosswise grainlines. (Fig. 1-7)

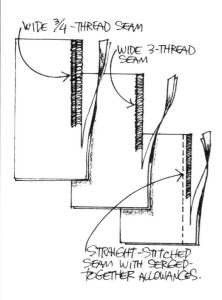

Fig. 1-7 Serge-seam with a wide stitch, or straight-stitch the seam and serge-finish the allowances together with a narrower stitch.

If puckering occurs, set the differential feed at 0.7. If you do not have differential feed on your machine, use taut serging—holding both layers taut in front of and behind the presser foot but being careful not to pull the fabric through the machine. (Fig. 1-8)

Fig. 1-8 Hold the fabric taut to prevent puckering.

Go—Begin with a Simple Pullover Top

1. Trim the neckline seam allowances to 1/4" if they were cut wider. With right sides together, serge-seam the right shoulder.

2. Pin the other shoulder at the seamline and test to make sure the top will fit over your head when finished. Trim out the front neckline edge, if necessary (see box). The finished neckline with the bias band application will be approximately the same measurement as the cut edge.

> **To enlarge the neckline, trim fabric from the center front to the shoulder seams. You may trim the shoulder area slightly but do not trim the back neckline. For this alteration, trim only 1/4" at a time and fit the opening over your head until it is the desired size. (Fig. 1-9)**
>
>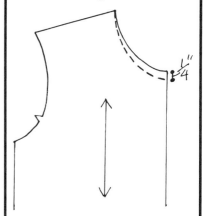
>
> Fig. 1-9 Trim the front neckline 1/4" at a time, tapering to the shoulder.

3. Fold the neckline band lengthwise with wrong sides together. With the band on the right side of the neckline opening and cut edges matching, serge-seam, trimming slightly to neaten.

Stretch the band slightly in the curved areas while serging. Trim the unattached end of the band.

4. Lightly press the band up and the seam allowance down toward the garment and, from the right side, top-stitch to secure. (Fig. 1-10)

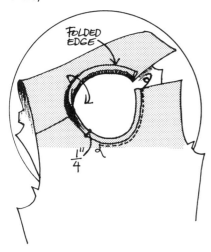

Fig. 1-10 After serging the folded band to the neckline, press the allowance toward the garment and top-stitch.

5. Serge-seam the other shoulder, matching the band and seamline. Press the shoulder seam allowances toward the back.

> **To neatly finish and secure the second shoulder seam at the neckline, top-stitch the shoulder allowance to the band from the right side. (Fig. 1-11)**

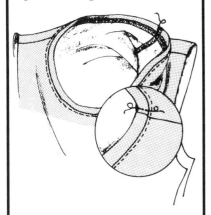

Fig. 1-11 Top-stitch the allowance to the band to neatly secure.

6. If you are planning to wear the top with shoulder pads, attach *Velcro* to hold them in place. On the wrong side, center a 3" *Velcro* strip (the soft side) on each shoulder seam. Stitch-in-the-ditch of the seam from the right side, catching the strip in the stitching.

7. With the garment on top, serge-seam the sleeves to the bodice. Press the seam allowance toward the sleeve. (Fig. 1-12)

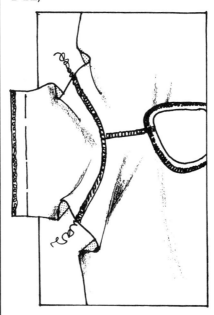

Fig. 1-12 Serge-seam the sleeves to the garment.

> **If the sleeve needs to be eased to the garment, the serger will automatically help. If your sleeve has a lot of ease, set the differential feed on 2.0. If you do not have differential feed, hold the top layer slightly taut above the lower layer, allowing the serger to ease in the fullness of the sleeve.**

8. Serge-finish the lower sleeve edges. Press up the sleeve hem allowances.

9. Serge one underarm seam from the lower hemline of the pullover body to the sleeve edge. Press the seam allowance toward the back.

10. Serge-finish the lower edge of the pullover.

11. Serge-seam the other underarm as in step 9. (Fig. 1-13)

Fig. 1-13 After serge-finishing the lower edge, serge the second underarm seam.

12. Press up the lower edge of the pullover and top-stitch all hems, catching the upper hem edges.

Serge Foolproof Pull-on Pants

1. For pants with side seams, serge-seam right sides together, front to back, serging from the lower edge to the waistline. Press the allowances toward the back. (For pants without side seams, begin with step 2.)

2. Serge-finish the lower edge of each leg.

3. Serge-seam the inseam on both legs. (Fig. 1-14) You do not need to cut the thread between the legs until you're finished.

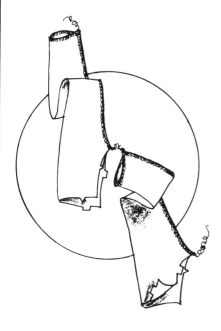

Fig. 1-14 Serge both inseams.

4. Turn one leg right side out and insert it inside the second leg. Matching the inseams, serge-seam the crotch.

5. Measure the elastic to fit your waistline comfortably. Overlap the ends 1/2" and secure by zigzagging.

6. Carefully fit the pants (see box) and serge-finish the upper edge.

Try on the pants and place the elastic around your waist. Mark the casing foldline. Test the accuracy of the crotch depth by folding and pinning the casing over the elastic and sitting. Trim any excess fabric before serge-finishing. (Fig. 1-15)

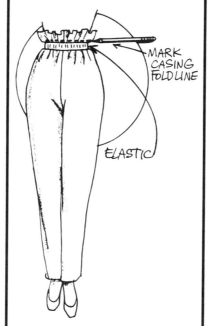

MARK CASING FOLDLINE

ELASTIC

Fig. 1-15 Try on the pants and place the elastic around your waist.

7. Press the casing to the wrong side along the foldline. Top-stitch the loose casing edge next to the elastic. (Fig. 1-16)

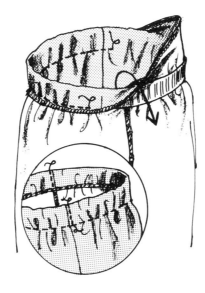

Fig. 1-16 Press the casing to the wrong side and top-stitch the loose casing edge.

---

8. Distribute the gathers over the elastic evenly. Stitch-in-the-ditch of the front and back seamlines and at the sides to secure the elastic and prevent it from rolling. (Straight-stitch through the elastic vertically at the sides even if your pattern has no side seams.)

Distribute the elastic evenly before stitching-in-the-ditch by stretching the opening to its maximum width and then releasing.

9. Top-stitch the leg hems in place.

NOTES

CHAPTER 2

PLANNING ANY PROJECT

Planning Any Project

Pattern Selection ✀ Fabric Considerations ✀ Fast Fitting ✀ Interfacing Choices ✀ Cutting and Marking
Testing ✀ When to Serge, When to Sew ✀ Construction Order

Pattern Selection

You'll need to consider several factors simultaneously when selecting a pattern for your serging project. The type and style of garment you want to make, how much time you have to spend on construction, and how you will utilize your serger in the construction process are all important. The serger techniques you will learn in this book can save time and allow you to professionally finish any garment.

If you plan to use your serger for most of the construction, a simple pattern with minimal lines and details will be the fastest and easiest. Most pattern companies identify their easiest patterns with a logo on the envelope. Several companies also have serger patterns which include specific serging instructions. (Fig. 2-1)

Easy-to-sew patterns are ideal for fast serging construction because they have few pattern pieces (meaning few seams), simple styling, and a relaxed fit or full cut (meaning fitting is not complicated). The easy-to-sew styles are often designed with time-saving dropped shoulders, elasticized waists, simply finished necklines, and machine-sewn hems. (Fig. 2-2)

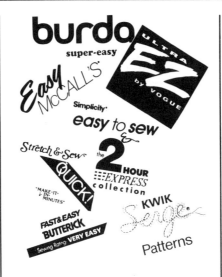

Fig. 2-1 Look for easy-to-sew logos from all the pattern companies to speed up your serging projects.

Serger patterns and some easy-to-sew patterns include serging instructions in the guidesheets. These may be integrated into the step-by-step instructions or may simply be given as general serging information separate from the conventional construction steps (such as options for hems and seam finishes). After you have read the remainder of this book, you'll want to decide for yourself the best techniques and construction order for every pattern before beginning the project. Even if the pattern includes "serger instructions," you may want to change some of the techniques and the sewing order.

Fig. 2-2 Simple patterns help make serged garment construction as fast as possible.

When selecting a pattern, ask these questions to help estimate how much time you'll need to spend on the garment and how effectively you can use the serger to speed up the process:

1. What type of fabric will I be using? (See discussion on this page.)

2. How much fitting will I need to do during construction? (Guidelines on page 12.)

3. What kind of seams will be best for my fabric and pattern? (Chapter 3 covers seam types.)

4. Can I effectively substitute serger techniques for all or many of the pattern's sewing techniques? (The remaining chapters in this book will help you make these decisions.)

5. How can I use the serger to quickly edge-finish or hem the garment?

The details on the pattern envelope will help you plan the garment construction. (Fig 2-3)

Fig. 2-3 Read the pattern envelope for a detailed garment description.

On the envelope back, the garment description describes the fit and lists features that may not be obvious on the envelope front, such as plackets, darts, lining, waistband, and type of sleeve.

Although features such as collars, cuffs, plackets, and zippers are usually not featured in the easy-to-sew patterns, serger techniques can be effectively used to speed up their sewing time. No matter whether the garment is simple or complex, the serger can be used to save time in the overall construction.

Fabric Considerations

Many serger enthusiasts have told us that they purchased their serger to sew knits. And yes, the serger does make knit sewing a breeze. But it can be used just as easily to professionally construct and finish practically any other fabric.

Time-saving serger techniques can be used effectively on any fabric but your choice of technique will vary according to the looseness or tightness of the fabric weave, the weight of the fabric, and the amount of wear and care the garment will receive.

The majority of serger techniques can be used on all of today's fabrics. However, a few techniques will not work well on some specialty fabrics, such as velvet or denim, which need particular handling. When unsure, always test first, before serging on the actual project. For complete information on serging

all of today's textiles, see *Simply Serge Any Fabric* listed under "Other Books by the Authors" at the back of this book.

When purchasing yardage for a serged garment, buy the amount specified on the pattern envelope. If you have already purchased your fabric, you may be able to get by with a little less. Save fabric by cutting out with 1/4" serged seam and hem allowances or plan to bind the edges. Eliminate facings by using a serge-finishing technique (see Chapters 4, 6, and 10) or totally lining the garment.

> **Also consider using another color of fabric for facings or for any garment section such as sleeves, pockets, or collars. You may choose to mix several fabrics in one garment or alter the fabric before cutting by serge-seaming a contrasting fabric inset or a color-blocked design.**

With the exception of ribbing, preshrink or pretreat your fabric before cutting out:

✂ Use the same method of care you will use for the finished garment, including using detergent for laundering. Most fabrics will shrink in the lengthwise direction, some up to 6" per yard.

✄ To prevent raveling while pretreating wovens, serge-finish the fabric ends first. (Fig. 2-4)

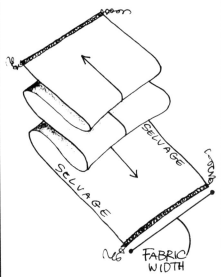

Fig. 2-4 Serge-finish the fabric ends before pretreating.

✄ Preshrink washable knits by laundering and drying twice. This will also help you to determine whether the fold crease will be permanent. If it does not come out in pretreatment, you will need to refold to avoid the crease when cutting out so it does not fall in a conspicuous area on your garment.

✄ While some fabrics may not shrink, pretreating is still helpful to remove finishes that may cause skipped or uneven stitches.

> Pretreat your fabric as soon as you bring it home from the store. This eliminates any guessing as to whether or not it has been pretreated when you are ready to use it and saves time when you're ready to begin a project.

Fast Fitting

Accurate fitting is important on any garment, but it is crucial when serging. A garment that is too large can be serged smaller, but a serged garment that is too tight cannot be easily altered.

Before buying a pattern, recheck your body measurements. Don't simply purchase a pattern according your ready-to-wear size. Instead, compare your measurements to the ones on the back of the pattern envelope and buy the size indicated. If your measurements are between sizes, purchase the next larger size.

> For most patterns, except those which have many design details or are very fitted, you'll usually need only five basic measurements for fitting: bust, waist, hip, center-back waist length, and finished length. Add the crotch length measurement when making pants. (Fig. 2-5)

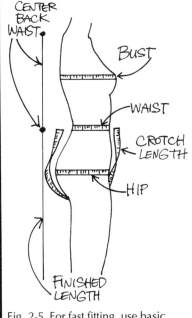

Fig. 2-5 For fast fitting, use basic measurements.

If you are sewing for a child, check the measurements each time you sew. Rapid growth causes sizes to change often. Keep in mind also that a child's head is larger in proportion to the body than an adult's.

Easy fitting tips:

✄ Choose patterns that are loose-fitting, especially when sewing with a woven fabric, because they will require the least adjustment.

✄ For tops and dresses, buy the pattern according to your bust measurement. For pants and skirts, buy according to your hip measurement. For full skirts, buy according to your waist measurement.

✄ Measure the length of a favorite finished garment in a similar style and compare that to the measurements on the pattern.

✄ Select a pattern that is multi-sized, especially if your bust size is a different size from waist or hips. (Fig. 2-6)

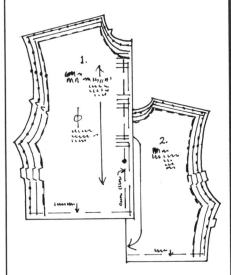

Fig. 2-6 Multisized patterns help you quickly fit a multisized figure.

When determining the finished pants length, measure the length of the outseam. Inseam lengths vary with the pant style. A tight-fitting pair of pants will have a longer inseam than looser-fitting trousers.

When checking your sleeve length, allow for the depth of the shoulder pads if you plan to wear them in your garment.

Make as many adjustments as possible to the pattern before cutting out the garment. Start by adjusting the length measurements beginning from the top of the garment and working down: center back waist, sleeve length, finished length from waist to lower edge, and crotch depth on a pants pattern. Be sure to make adjustments to both the front and back pattern pieces. (Fig. 2-7)

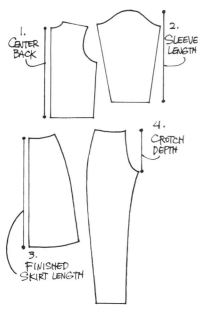

Fig. 2-7 Make length adjustments from the top of the garment down.

Make any length adjustments at the shorten/lengthen line on the pattern pieces. Adjusting at the lower edge of a shaped pattern piece will change the circumference of the edge as well as changing the length of a placket opening or skirt vent.

Next adjust the width measurements on the pattern, comparing your measurements to those on the pattern envelope. (Fig. 2-8)

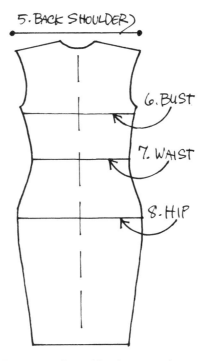

Fig. 2-8 Make width adjustments last.

As a double check, measure the pattern pieces to determine if they are adequate for your measurements plus any desired ease. Some patterns are labeled with finished measurements on the bust and hip lines, eliminating the need to measure the pattern piece. Make any width adjustments evenly on both sides of the garment.

Most patterns have built-in wearing ease. Check the back pages of the pattern catalog for the amount of ease the company has included in each pattern. Minimum ease standards allow for 2-1/2" at the bust, 1" at the waist, 3" at the hip, and 2" at the upper arm.

It is not necessary to adjust a pattern if your measurements vary 1/8" or less from the pattern measurements. For loose-fitting garments, variances up to 1" of the bust measurement will not need adjustment. If a blouse or top is not fitted at the waistline, do not bother with the center back waist adjustment. Lengthen at the lower edge instead. (Fig. 2-9)

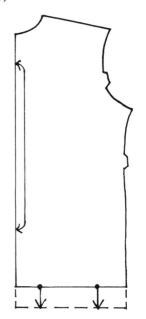

Fig. 2-9 For a nonfitted waistline, make the center back waistline adjustment at the lower edge.

Knits-only patterns, especially those for two-way stretch fabrics, may allow for little or no ease, or even minus ease. Special occasion garments, such as wedding dresses or formals, may have little or no ease. For these patterns, warnings against too-tight fitting may be printed on the bodice pattern pieces.

Where you are unsure about length or width measurements, add for a 1"- to 1-1/2"-wide seam allowance to ensure adequate ease.

> **Make a notation of any pattern adjustments or garment alterations and the date they were made. Include these in the pattern envelope for the next time you use the pattern.**

For additional fitting insurance:

✀ Pin-fit the pattern before cutting out.

✀ Determine the type of seaming you will use in your garment. Serge-finishing the seam allowance edges and then straight-stitching the seam will leave the allowances in place for any needed alteration. Or machine-baste with a serger chainstitch if you have that capability on your machine.

> **If you straight-stitch the seam, then serge-finish the allowances together, serge without trimming anything off the edge. The width will remain accurate and any necessary alterations can still be made. (Fig. 2-10)**

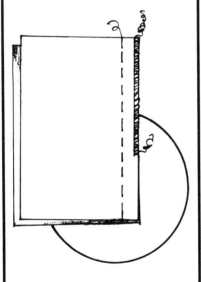

Fig. 2-10 To allow alteration room, serge-finish the allowances together without trimming.

✀ Machine-baste major seams before serging. After fitting, serge-seam over the basting. Remove any basting stitches that show on the right side of the garment. If you need to take in the garment, merely serge-seam a deeper seam without bothering to take out the basting. (Fig. 2-11)

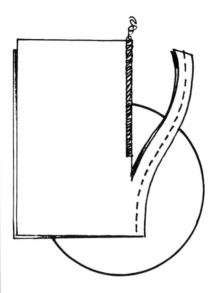

Fig. 2-11 Serge-seam inside the basting to take in the garment.

> **For fast removal of machine-basting stitches, loosen the needle tension before basting. The stitches can then be easily removed by pulling out the bobbin thread. Another option is to use *Wash-away* thread for basting any washable fabrics. It will hold the garment together temporarily but is easily removed by spraying with water.**

Interfacing Choices

With the wide variety of interfacings available, it is often difficult to select the right one for your fabric and garment. An interfacing may be either fusible or sew-in. Check your pattern envelope or guidesheet for information. Some patterns even give a listing of specific name brands to assist you. (Fig. 2-12)

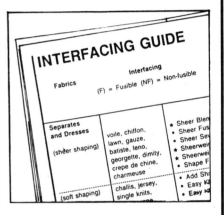

Fig. 2-12 Look for interfacing information on the pattern envelope or guidesheet.

Fusible interfacing requires the least amount of effort for application and is our choice for most garments. Fusibles come in various weights and types—woven, nonwoven, knit, warp-insertion, and weft-insertion. Choose an interfacing that is lighter weight than the fabric because the fusing material tends to add weight after it is applied.

Always test several interfacings by fusing swatches on scraps of your garment fabric. Study each to see if the interfacing fuses properly and is not visible from the right side of the fabric. (Fig. 2-13) Fusibles can be used with most fabrics, with a few exceptions. Heat- or steam-sensitive fabrics, very tightly woven fabrics, fabrics with finishes such as water repellency, and puckered, napped, or pile fabrics may need sew-in interfacing.

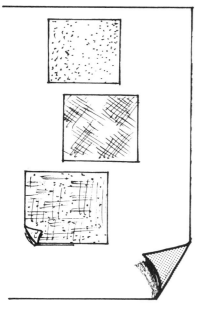

Fig. 2-13 Fuse interfacing swatches to the fabric to check for best results.

For knit fabrics, select a fusible knit interfacing which will stretch and recover with the stretch of the knit.

If a fusible interfacing is not compatible with your fabric, use one of the many varieties of sew-in interfacings. Consider using self-fabric to interface soft and sheer fabrics. Chapter 3 covers serging techniques for both types of interfacing.

Store fusible interfacing by folding it carefully or rolling it on a tube to prevent wrinkling. Wrinkles won't press out during application and may cause inadequate fusing. Store the interleaf (giving the identification and instructions) with the interfacing. The application method will vary with different types of fusibles. (Fig. 2-14)

Fig. 2-14 Store fusible interfacing with the interleaf.

To save time, preshrink fusible interfacing during application. Press the fabric where the interfacing will be applied. Position the interfacing on the wrong side of the garment piece, resin side down. Holding the steam iron about 1" above the interfacing, steam generously to shrink and then fuse it to the fabric. (Fig. 2-15)

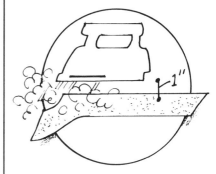

Fig. 2-15 Steam-shrink fusible interfacing generously, then fuse it to the fabric.

For this preshrinking step, it is important to use an iron which gives plenty of steam. If you use fusibles often, a press, available from several of the sewing-machine companies, is invaluable. It speeds up the fusing process, as well as applying greater pressure for the best possible fused bond. (Fig. 2-16)

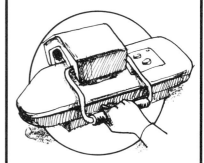

Fig. 2-16 A press speeds up fusing and helps perfect the bond.

Cutting and Marking

Follow these time-saving techniques to speed up your serged garment construction:

✄ For easiest and fastest cutting of woven fabrics, use a rotary cutter and mat. Pattern weights also save the time of pinning the pattern to the fabric.

✄ To control slippage of silky fabrics, lay out and cut the fabric on the flannel side of a vinyl tablecloth; or secure the fabric to a cardboard cutting mat by pinning the seam allowances to the mat. (Fig. 2-17)

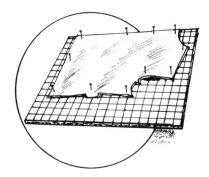

Fig. 2-17 Pin slippery fabric to a cardboard cutting mat.

✄ When using 1/4" seam allowances, cut all notches out beyond the allowances to avoid weakening the seams. For 5/8" allowances, clip in 1/8" at the notch markings (this still allows for alterations, if necessary). Use 1/8" clip marks for hemlines and folds such as facings or pleats. After clipping, fold on the clip marks and press the fabric into position. Remember that notches and clips will be trimmed away during serging. (Fig. 2-18)

✄ Use water-soluble or air-erasable marking pens for fast and easy markings. Test on fabric scraps before marking the

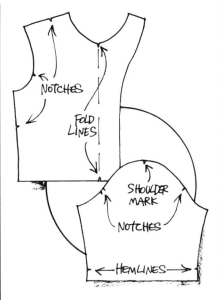

Fig. 2-18 With 5/8" allowances, make 1/8" clip marks.

garment pieces. As a safety factor, always mark with small dots on the wrong side of the fabric. Keep in mind that air-erasable markings disappear quickly, so mark right before you plan to sew.

✄ Use *Pattern Pals* to mark fabrics that may be damaged by other types of markings. These pressure-sensitive symbols can be placed on the fabric during cutting and then easily removed during construction. (Fig. 2-19)

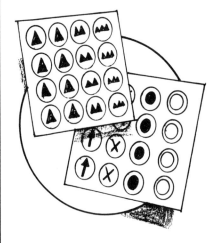

Fig. 2-19 Press-on *Pattern Pals* help with difficult marking chores.

Testing

After cutting, it is important to test your serging using a size 11/75 needle on scraps of your garment fabric—on both the crosswise and lengthwise grainlines. They will often react differently. Test the stitch length and width, tension settings, and differential feed adjustment. You may also want to test serging on the bias if any seamlines are in that direction. Remember to test with two layers of fabric if you are serge-seaming or serge-finishing the seam allowances together. (Fig. 2-20)

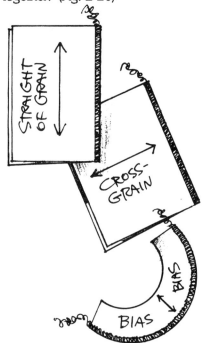

Fig. 2-20 Test and adjust your serging for the number of layers and direction of grain you'll use on the garment.

> **Be sure to test pressing the fabric, too. Use an iron temperature appropriate for your fabric. In many cases, you'll also need to use a press cloth.**

Snags or pulls in silky fabrics or holes in knits (especially *Lycra*-blend knits) may occur while you are test-serging. To prevent this, change to a new needle when you begin your project.

When to Serge, When to Sew

After testing serged stitching on your garment fabric, you will be better able to evaluate which techniques to use on the project. You will usually need to use both your serger and sewing machine for the most professional results.

In the remainder of this book, you will learn many techniques which combine sewing and serging. You'll be able to choose from several options for most applications. The pattern, fabric, your serging experience, and time available are all factors in the decision.

Here are some general guidelines for deciding when to serge and when to sew:

✂ Consider the fabric weight. Seams in heavy fabric such as wool are less bulky if the allowances are serge-finished and the seam is straight-stitched and pressed open. Most lightweight fabrics such as silkies, sheers, and laces can be serge-seamed nicely. (Fig. 2-21)

✂ The type of fabric is also important. Knit garments can usually be serge-seamed, no matter how tight. Woven garments should be serge-seamed only if they are loose-fitting.

✂ When you're unsure of the fit on any garment, always use wide serge-finished and straight-stitched seams.

✂ For some garments, such as better suits and dresses, the garment should be seamed and hemmed conventionally, using the serger for finishing only. The seamline can be pressed flatter, and the weight of pressed-open seams and wider hems enhances the drape and gives a professionally tailored appearance.

✂ For the best ease control, such as when setting in a shaped sleeve cap, the sewing machine is more accurate. You'll also use the sewing machine for tight curves and corners, top-stitching, and a conventional zipper application. (Fig. 2-22)

✂ Serging automatically trims an enclosed seam (used when applying a facing or on the inside of a lapel or collar) and saves the time of grading the allowances. On very fine fabric, however, the bulkier serged allowance may be too obvious.

✂ Study designer fashions and better ready-to-wear for innovative serging and sewing techniques.

Construction Order

Save time and prevent frustration by planning the construction order of your garment in advance. Whether you want to use your serger exclusively on a project or merely for finishing seam allowances, preplanning is essential.

The guidesheets of most patterns, with the exception of some serger patterns, do not change the traditional sewing order. But following a few simple guidelines, any guidesheet can be modified for the fastest and easiest serging and sewing.

In Chapter 1, you learned the fastest construction order for a basic pullover top and pull-on pants. Any garment can be made following a variation of those steps.

1. After testing, decide what type of seams and edge-finishes you will use on the garment.

2. Decide if you will incorporate any decorative serging in the garment and at what step.

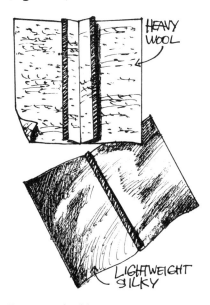

Fig. 2-21 The fabric weight will help determine the type of seams to use.

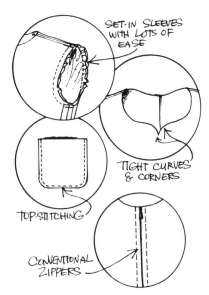

Fig. 2-22 The sewing machine should be used for some techniques.

3. Select appropriate techniques for constructing the garment (such as sleeve application, plackets, cuffs, collars, pockets, closures, waistline treatment, finishing touches).

4. Look over the pattern guidesheet for any additional sewing steps that can be converted to serging.

5. Determine the most efficient order of construction, and mark the guidesheet to reflect any changes. (Fig. 2-23)

Fig. 2-23 Plan the most time-saving construction order and change the guidesheet.

For the speediest construction order, keep in mind the following:

✂ Consolidate steps which require the same serging stitch, such as a rolled edge or decorative serging.

✂ Group steps which use the same thread and thread color.

✂ Whenever possible, serge pieces flat rather than sewing in a circle. For the fastest hems, eliminate any slits and serge-finish the edge continuously. (Fig. 2-24)

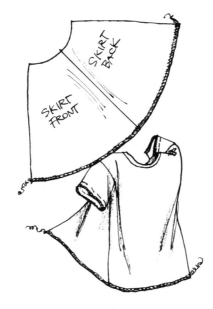

Fig. 2-24 Serge on a flat garment section when possible.

> **After serge-finishing a flat sleeve edge or hem that will be turned and top-stitched later, press up the hem allowance while it is still flat. This is much easier than turning up the hem after the edge has been serge-seamed into a circle.**

✂ Do detail work such as pockets and zippers on flat garment sections whenever possible.

✂ Serge as many seams and edges as possible continuously, without raising the presser foot. Chain for 4" to 6" between the pieces so the stitching won't pull apart when the thread is clipped to separate the pieces. (Fig. 2-25)

Fig. 2-25 Serge-seam and serge-finish continuously, when possible, to speed up the process.

✂ Group the serging steps, the sewing steps, and pressing, too, for the most efficiency and speed.

✂ On tops, you'll usually serge-seam or sew one or both shoulder seams and finish the neckline edge before finishing and applying the sleeves and completing the garment.

✂ On bottoms, you'll most often partially seam to finish the hem edge flat, then finish seaming and complete the waistline treatment. Apply a zipper flat before completing the seaming.

CHAPTER 3

SERGER CONSTRUCTION BASICS

Serger Construction Basics

Prepare to Serge ✂ Seam Types ✂ Serged-Seam Pointers ✂ Reinforced Seams
Negotiating Corners and Curves ✂ Serging Darts ✂ Fast Interfacing Techniques

Prepare to Serge

Before you sit down to serge any project, be sure your machine is in the best possible working condition and follow a few simple guidelines, as outlined below.

Check the needle(s)—Rub your finger over the end of the needle (or both needles on a 2-needle model) to see if it is blunt, bent, or burred. If in doubt, throw away the old needle and change to a new (sharp) needle to prevent any damage to the fabric.

> **When serging knits, always start with a new needle to prevent holes which can show up next to the seamline and grow larger with wear. (Fig. 3-1)**

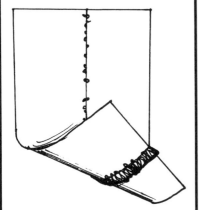

Fig. 3-1 When serging knits, use a sharp new needle to eliminate holes along the needleline.

> **For serging microfiber fabric (which is made of very fine polyester filaments, looks and feels like silk, and has the durability and care requirements of a synthetic), use a new smaller size needle to prevent snagging the closely woven, fine fibers. You may need to change needles several times during construction because the fibers dull the needle quickly.**

Keep extra needles of different sizes on hand. You'll need larger needles for serging heavier fabrics or when using heavier thread for some flatlocking.

> **If conventional sewing-machine needles are used in your serger, you may get a better stitch quality with the brand your dealer recommends. For example, if *Organ* needles were supplied with your serger, continue to buy and use them to ensure perfect serged stitching.**

Clean the machine—After every project you should clean the lint and trimmings from your serger to prevent buildup and potential damage. If you didn't clean your machine after your last project, do so before beginning the next one. Also oil the machine if it needs it (if it hasn't been used for several months or if you've serged for over 12 to 15 hours since you last oiled it). Consult your owner's manual for instructions.

> **Make a habit of keeping your serger in top-notch condition. Once a month, check the knives and clean thoroughly around the machine workings and knives and between the tension discs. At least once a year, take your serger to a serger repair specialist for a checkup and retiming.**

Select the thread—When serging lightweight fabrics, use lighter-weight serger or machine-embroidery thread for less bulky seams. On fabrics with any show-through, match your thread color to the fabric so it will be less visible from the right side. When possible, use matching thread on any seam so the inside of your garment is as professionally finished as the outside.

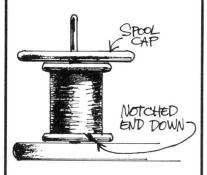

Fig. 3-2 Take precautions with conventional spools to prevent stitching problems.

Pin with caution—It is not always necessary to pin when using a serger because the longer presser foot holds the fabric in position. If you do need to pin, it is important to place the pins so that they will not be hit by the knives. Hitting a pin can damage one or both of the knives, and can also put the serger out of timing.

Place the pins parallel to the stitching line to the left of the seamline for the safest method. On fabrics that will be damaged by pinning, such as leathers and velvets, place the pins in the seam allowance. When pinning in the seam allowance, watch carefully and remove the pins before they reach the presser foot. (Fig. 3-3)

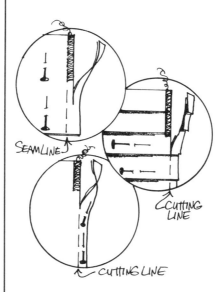

Fig. 3-3 When pinning is necessary, pin to the left of the seamline or outside the cutting line.

Another pinning option is to place the pins horizontal to the seam at the left of the needle, out of the range of the knives. This method works best for pleats and tucks and for other tricky procedures such as applying ribbing and elastic.

To avoid losing pins when working on sweatering or textured fabric, use large-headed pins, such as floral or hat pins, for best visibility.

Baste for perfection—To check the fit of a garment, to match stripes, or to handle slippery fabrics, you may choose to baste instead of pinning. Basting options include machine-basting, hand-basting, or using basting tape or glue. When using basting tape, position it on the edge of the seam allowance or to the left of the stitching line to avoid stitching or cutting through it. Use glue sparingly and in the seam allowances only.

When serge-seaming striped fabric, allow a scant 1/8" of the underlayer of the fabric to show so you can match the stripes as you serge, without basting. (Fig. 3-4)

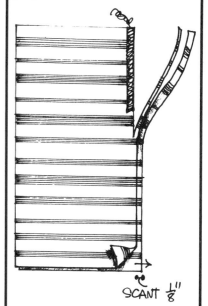

Fig. 3-4 To match stripes without basting, let the under layer extend slightly.

Seam Types

With your serger, you have a wide range of seaming options. You can use the serger exclusively when seaming, or you can use serging in tandem with conventional straight-stitching. Serged seams can be decoratively featured on the outside of your garment, or they can be hidden on the inside. The type you select will depend on your fabric and garment styling (as discussed in Chapter 2) as well as on your personal taste and preference.

Decorative seaming is discussed in detail in *ABCs of Serging* and the *Know Your Serger* series (see "Other Books by the Authors" in the back of this book). Any seam with the serged allowances on the outside of the garment can be decorative. A wide variety of decorative seams are possible by varying the stitch type, length, and width; the type and color of thread; and the technique used.

> When the serging is exposed decoratively, the stitch should be uniform and attractive. Serge in the same direction as much as possible. For a heightened effect, shorten the stitch length and use decorative thread (select one that will be durable).

Hidden seaming, as opposed to decorative seaming, positions the allowances on the inside of the garment where they won't be seen. Many seam types can be serged either hidden or decorative, depending on the look you are trying to achieve.

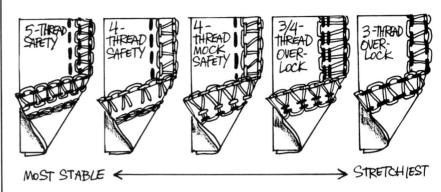

BASIC SERGED SEAMS:

5-THREAD SAFETY · 4-THREAD SAFETY · 4-THREAD MOCK SAFETY · 3/4-THREAD OVER-LOCK · 3-THREAD OVERLOCK

MOST STABLE ←————————————→ STRETCHIEST

Fig. 3-5 Any balanced 3-, 4-, or 5-thread stitch can be used for serge-seaming.

Serged seams

Basic serged seam—Most balanced serged stitches can be used for seaming, and the speedy serger does the seaming, trimming, and finishing all in one step. Serged seaming may be used on any width seam allowance. Serged stitches vary in stability from the 5-thread, which is the most stable and allows very little, if any, stretch, to the 3-thread, which has the most stretch. (Fig. 3-5)

Select the stitch width and length to use in a serged seam based upon the weight and weave of your fabric.

Serged Seam Guidelines

Fabric	Width	Length	Stitch
Lightweight, tightly woven silkies, sheers, lingerie	Narrow to medium	Medium (short to medium for decorative)	3-thread
Mediumweight, tightly woven cottons, blends, and stable knits	Medium to wide	Medium (Short to medium for decorative)	3-, 3/4-, or 4-thread mock safety
Loosely woven mediumweight fabrics; stretch Lycra fabrics; sweatering, ribbing, and elastics	Wide	Medium to long (Short to medium for decorative)	3-, 3/4-, or 4-thread mock safety
Loosely woven fabrics with no stretch required; fabrics which require stable seams	Wide	Medium to long	4- or 5-thread safety

A 3- or 3/4-thread balanced stitch works well for seaming knits (even minus-ease swimwear and exercisewear) because the stitching stretches with the fabric. Test serged seams on knits by stretching them as they will be stretched when worn. If a thread or threads break, it is usually the needle thread(s). Try loosening the tension slightly or stretch the fabric a little when serge-seaming (if it doesn't distort the seam).

To prevent stretched-out seams on some knit fabrics, adjust the differential feed to 2.0, or ease-plus manually as you serge. To ease-plus, hold your finger behind the presser foot and force-feed the fabric in front of the presser foot. (Fig. 3-6)

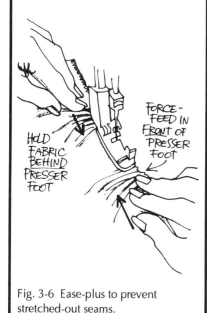

Fig. 3-6 Ease-plus to prevent stretched-out seams.

Top-stitched serged seam—To secure the seam allowance of a wider serged seam, press it to one side and top-stitch with a straight-stitch, twin-needle, or decorative stitch. (Fig. 3-7)

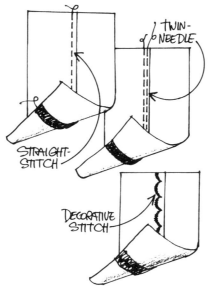

Fig. 3-7 Top-stitch the serged allowance to one side for stability and decorative detail.

Rolled-edge seam—Sheers and lightweight fabrics may be seamed using the rolled-edge stitch. Test to be sure the seam does not pull away from the fabric. You may need to widen the stitch (if possible on your model) for more seam stability. (Fig. 3-8)

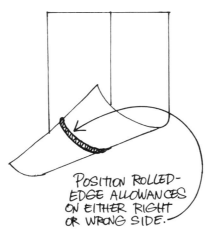

Fig. 3-8 Use a rolled-edge stitch to seam sheers and lightweight fabrics.

Hairline seam—To make a hairline seam on loosely woven, lightweight, or sheer fabric (where the serging may pull away from the material), place the fabric right sides together and serge-seam using a narrow balanced stitch over a strip of bias tricot such as *Seams Great*. After serge-seaming, carefully trim away the remaining tricot. (Fig. 3-9)

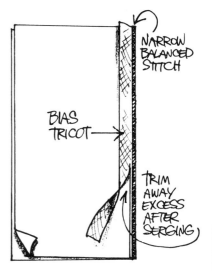

Fig. 3-9 Serge a hairline seam on loosely woven, lightweight, or sheer fabric.

Flatlocked seam—In flatlock seaming, the stitching is always exposed on both sides of the fabric. Flatlocking was developed to replicate an industrial cover stitch, which is a popular look in ready-to-wear sportswear and lingerie. For flatlocked seams:

✄ Most often you'll use the widest 3-thread flatlock. (A 2-thread flatlock can be used for delicate or lightweight seaming.)

✄ Always allow the stitches to hang off the edges when flatlocking so they can be pulled flat. (Fig. 3-10)

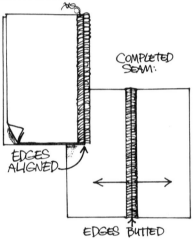

Fig. 3-10 Flatlock-seam with the stitching halfway off the edge.

✄ Serge with wrong sides together to position the loops on the right side. Serge with right sides together to feature the ladder stitch on the right side.

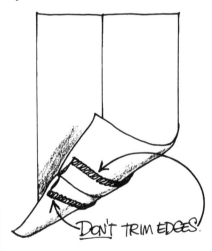

Fig. 3-11 Add durability to flatlocking by serge-finishing, folding, or seaming first.

For more durable flatlock seaming, try the options listed below:

✄ Serge-finish the edges separately with a narrow balanced stitch and flatlock with a wide stitch.

✄ Serge-finish the seam allowances and fold them to the wrong side. Flatlock over the folded edges.

✄ Serge-finish the seam allowances and straight-stitch the seam. With wrong sides together, flatlock over the seam. (Fig. 3-11)

Straight-stitched seams

Straight-stitching with serge-finished seam allowances produces a durable seam with wider allowances. If you are uncertain about fit, use one of the straight-stitched and serge-finished seaming techniques. Also consider a straight-stitched seam if you are using a heavy fabric or when you prefer the drape and durability of such a seam.

Serge-finished and straight-stitched seam—After cutting out a garment, first serge-finish the seam-allowance edges. Then straight-stitch the seam using a 5/8" allowance and press the seam open. (Fig. 3-12) Some tips:

Fig. 3-12 Serge-finish the allowances before straight-stitching the seam.

✄ Serge-finish by just skimming the edges with the knives. Serging more than this amount can change the fit of your garment when a standard seam-allowance width is used.

✄ Serge-finish using continuous serging, chaining off one piece for approximately 4" and serging onto the next garment piece without raising the presser foot (see Fig. 2-25).

✂ With loosely woven fabric, serge-finish immediately after cutting to prevent raveling and fraying during construction.

When serge-finishing an unlined jacket, serge-finish from the right side of the fabric with a contrasting color of decorative thread. Use a narrow satin-length stitch to give the appearance of a narrow binding. Experiment with different threads and stitch widths for the best effect. (Fig. 3-13)

Fig. 3-13 Your serge-finishing will look like a binding when you use a short, narrow stitch.

Straight-stitched and top-stitched seam—Press open the seam allowance after serge-finishing the edges and straight-stitching on the seamline. Top-stitch the seam allowances in place to secure them and add decorative detail. (Fig. 3-14)

✂ After pressing the seam allowances open, top-stitch 1/4" to 3/8" from the seamline on both sides using a straight, zigzag, or decorative stitch.

✂ Top-stitch directly over the pressed-open seamline using a twin-needle. The wider 4mm needle produces the most durable stitch.

✂ Top-stitch next to or directly over the pressed-open seamline using a decorative stitch.

Straight-stitched with allowances serge-finished together— On lighter-weight fabrics only, straight-stitch on the 5/8" seamline, then serge-finish the seam allowances together, trimming approximately 1/4". (Fig. 3-15)

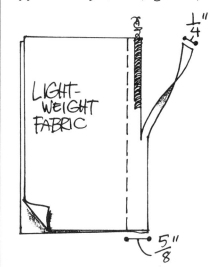

Fig. 3-15 On lighter-weight fabrics, straight-stitch the seam before serge-finishing the allowances together.

When applying this type of straight-stitched seam on knit fabric, seam with a twin-needle (or use a narrow zigzag stitch if a twin-needle is unavailable) for added stretch along the seamline. Then serge-finish the allowances together. (Fig. 3-16)

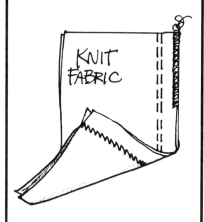

Fig. 3-16 For stretchability, seam with a twin-needle before serge-finishing.

If you're using a straight-stitched and serged-together stitch on loosely woven fabric, serge the allowances together with a medium-to-wide balanced stitch, barely skimming the edges. With the wider allowances, the seam looks and functions much like a 5-thread serged seam. (Fig. 3-17)

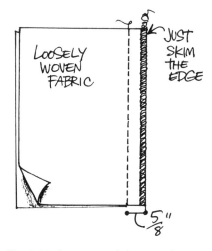

Fig. 3-17 For more stability, straight-stitch the seam, then serge-finish using a medium-to-wide stitch.

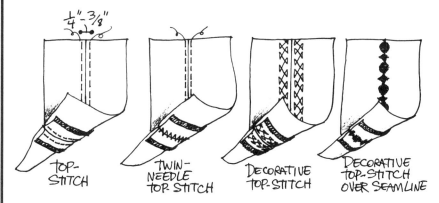

Fig. 3-14 After seaming, top-stitch to decoratively secure the allowances.

Combination seams

Several useful seam types combine serging and sewing. Each works well for specific applications. Often on combination seams, the seam allowances are enclosed. These were designed to keep the serged allowances from showing (on some tailored or reversible garments) and to add stability and durability.

Serged flat-felled seam—A serged flat-felled seam is a simple, durable, professional finish for denims, canvas, and other heavier fabrics. It is used sometimes as a sporty seam-finish on lighter-weight fabrics such as chambray and broadcloth. Although this seam resembles the time-consuming flat-felled seam traditionally used on ready-to-wear denim garments, it can be serged much faster. (Fig. 3-18)

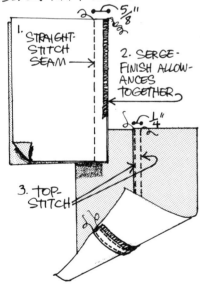

Fig. 3-18 Combine straight-stitching and serging for a durable, sporty seam.

1. Straight-stitch with a 5/8" seam allowance and right sides together.

2. Serge-finish the seam allowances together with a medium-width, medium-length, balanced 3-thread stitch, just skimming the edges. Press the allowances to one side.

3. From the right side, top-stitch next to the seamline and again 1/4" away with matching or contrasting-color thread.

For less bulk when applying serged flat-felled seams on heavier fabrics, straight-stitch the seam and trim the under layer to 1/4". Serge-finish the upper allowance. Press the seam to one side and top-stitch as in step 3. (Fig. 3-19)

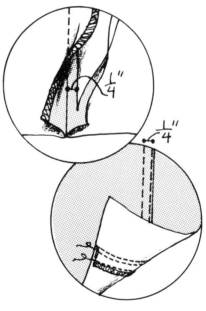

Fig. 3-19 Reduce bulk by trimming the under allowance before top-stitching.

Serged French seam—This seam resembles a traditional French seam both in appearance and technique. But the serger sews and trims in one step, eliminating tedious trimming of the seam allowances after straight-stitching. Used for lightweight fabrics, the serged French seam is an excellent choice for sheers and laces where the seam may show through to the right side of the garment. (Fig. 3-20)

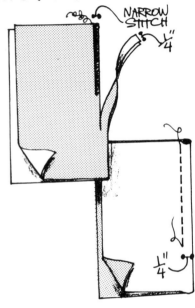

Fig. 3-20 Serge a French seam to hide the serged stitching on sheers and lace.

1. With wrong sides together, serge-seam using a narrow, medium-length, balanced 3-thread stitch and trimming about 1/4".

2. Carefully press open the seam. With right sides together, fold on the seamline, enclosing the serged allowance. Press carefully.

3. Straight-stitch 1/4" from the seam. Press the bound seam allowance to one side.

For a wider French seam variation, serge-seam with a 1/4" seam allowance and right sides together. Press, enclosing the seam. Straight-stitch 3/8" from the serged allowances. Press to one side and top-stitch close to the folded edge to secure. (Fig. 3-21) This seaming technique works well for a reversible garment when you don't want exposed serged seams. If you prefer the seams on the wrong side of the garment, serge-seam originally with wrong sides together.

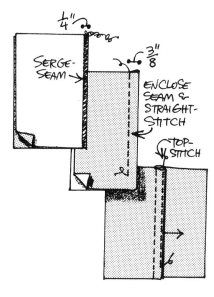

Fig. 3-21 Feature a wider French seam on the outside, with top-stitching to secure and flatten the allowance.

Enclosed serged seam—Designed for lightweight reversibles, this self-enclosed seam looks like a serged flat-felled seam from one side and a top-stitched seam from the other. The allowances are hidden inside. (Fig. 3-22)

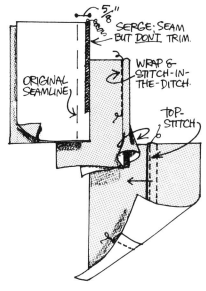

Fig. 3-22 Enclose a serged seam on lightweight reversibles.

1. Begin with 5/8" allowances. With right sides together, serge-seam, using the widest medium-length balanced stitch and barely skimming the edges. (You will not be stitching on the seamline.)

2. Press the serged seam to one side. Wrap the fabric tightly around the serged seam to enclose it and stitch-in-the-ditch to secure.

3. Press the enclosed seam allowances to the side, covering the seamline. Top-stitch along the folded edge.

Bound seam—Binding a seam adds durability and attractively finishes the inside of a garment. Traditional bound seams are quite time-consuming, but with the serger, you can make them easily. Use a strip of self-fabric for the binding or add interest with a contrasting color or fabric. Consider combinations such as satin to bind velvet or wool, and a nylon/*Lycra* binding on denim. (Fig. 3-23)

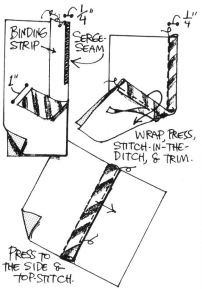

Fig. 3-23 Bind seam allowances for durability and an attractive finish.

1. For a 1/4" finished serged binding, cut a strip 1" wide. (The finished width of the binding will be slightly wider than your serger's widest stitch.) Cut the binding strip on the crosswise grain if the seam to be bound is straight. For curved seams, cut woven binding on the bias or knit binding in the direction of greatest stretch (usually crossgrain).

2. Trim the seam allowances you'll be binding to 1/4".

3. With the right sides of the garment together, align the strip over the seam allowances, matching the cut edges. Serge-seam using the widest medium-length balanced 3- or 3/4-thread stitch.

4. Wrap the binding around the seam, press, and stitch-in-the-ditch.

5. Trim the unfinished long edge of the binding close to the stitching on the underside.

6. Press the binding to the side, over the trimmed area, and top-stitch next to the folded edge.

To make a wider binding that resembles a strap seam, trim the seam allowances to 1/4". Cut a 1"-wide binding strip. Aligning the raw edges, serge-seam as described in the previous step 3. Fold the strap over the serged seam, enclosing it. Press under the binding raw edge 1/4" and top-stitch to secure. (Fig. 3-24)

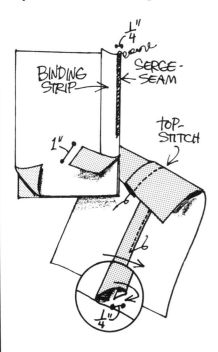

Fig. 3-24 Create a wider binding similar to a strap seam.

Lapped seam—Often featured on heavier fabrics and reversible garments, lapped seams are the flattest seams possible. Any width seam allowance can be used for this decoratively serged-finished seam. (Fig. 3-25)

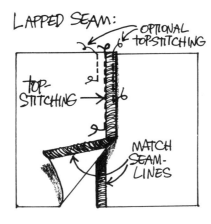

Fig. 3-25 Use a lapped seam on heavy fabrics and reversibles.

1. Using decorative or matching thread in the upper looper, serge-finish one seam allowance (or both allowances, if serging a reversible garment). Serge from the right side of the fabric, using a wide, short, balanced 3-thread stitch. Serge with the needle on the seamline, trimming off the excess seam allowance.

2. Lap the seam allowance edges, with the needlelines matching (and the decorative thread on the top if the garment isn't reversible).

3. Top-stitch along the needle-lines, through both layers. For more durability, you may want to top-stitch again along the seam-allowance edge on each side of the fabric.

Lapped-and-enclosed seam—This seam uses the lapped technique previously described but also encloses the serge-finished edges. Cut 3/4"-wide seam allowances to allow for enough fabric to enclose the seams. (Fig. 3-26)

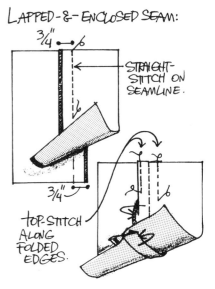

Fig. 3-26 To enclose the edges of a lapped seam, cut wider allowances, turn them under after seaming, and top-stitch to secure.

1. Serge-finish the seam allowances, just skimming the edge.

2. Lap as described in the previous step 2, matching and straight-stitching the layers together along the seamlines.

3. Fold both serged edges under 1/4" and top-stitch to secure.

Bound and lapped seam—
Another good choice for reversibles, this seam features bound edges, which are lapped and straight-stitched together. The binding can either match or contrast with the fabric. The binding can be as wide as your widest serged stitch. Use a narrower width for a more delicate or piped effect. (Fig. 3-27)

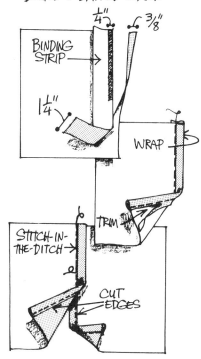

Fig. 3-27 Bind the edges with matching or contrasting fabric on this reversible seam.

1. Cut two 1-1/4"-wide bias strips the length of the seam.

2. Trim the seam allowances to 1/4" or trim with the knives while serge-seaming the binding to each allowance, right sides together.

> **If you are using a reversible fabric for this technique, serge-seam opposite or contrasting sides right sides together for a contrasting binding. For a matching binding, place the same sides together.**

3. After serge-seaming the binding, wrap the strip tightly around the serged allowances and stitch-in-the-ditch. Trim close to the stitching on the underside.

4. Lap the bound edges, matching the seamlines and sandwiching the trimmed binding edges between the two layers. Stitch-in-the-ditch over the previous stitching to complete the seam. Press flat.

Serged-Seam Pointers

✄ If you want the seam allowances hidden on the inside of the garment, sew or serge with right sides together. To position decorative seams on the outside of the garment, seam with wrong sides together.

✄ When easing one layer of fabric to another, as when inserting a sleeve or stretching one layer to another (when applying elastic or ribbing), always sew or serge with the longer layer underneath. The feed dogs will ease the under layer of fabric to the upper layer. Also set the differential feed at 2.0 and hold the upper layer taut to allow the serger to ease the under layer even more.

> **If you have a lot of fabric to ease in, raise the upper layer of fabric several inches above the under layer in front of the foot when serging or sewing. You may be able to ease in several inches using this technique. (Fig. 3-28)**

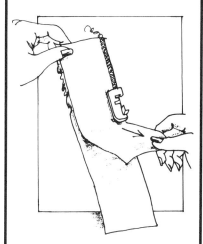

Fig. 3-28 To ease a bottom layer of fabric, raise the top layer and hold it taut.

✄ Pressing a serged or serge-finished seam can leave a ridge on the right side of the fabric. To prevent this, press carefully, using a sleeveboard or placing plain brown paper under the serged or serge-finished allowances.

✄ In most cases during garment construction, seam ends automatically will be secured when a seam or edge-finish crosses another seam. When seam ends will not be crossed and need to be secured, the fastest method is to use seam sealant. If the sealant is worn next to the skin, however, it can be irritating. In that case, thread the chain back through the stitching to secure, instead of using sealant.

✂ You can easily remove serged stitching by seaming again inside the stitching line, cutting off the original row, or by pulling the needle thread to release the stitching. In balanced serged stitching, the needle thread is the shortest thread in the chain. Find it and pull, sliding the fabric along it until the other threads are no longer secured and fall away from the fabric. (Fig. 3-29)

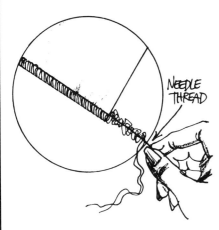

Fig. 3-29 Remove serged stitching by pulling the shortest thread in the chain.

If you feel you may have to remove the stitching for any reason, slightly loosen your needle thread tension(s) when serge-seaming or serge-finishing using a balanced stitch. When flatlocking, loosening and pulling the lower looper threads (the shortest in that stitch) will release the stitching.

Reinforced Seams

Stabilizing or reinforcing serged seams is usually unnecessary. However, on loosely woven fabrics and some stretch fabrics and on certain garment areas, seams and edges need to be reinforced.

If a serged seam is on an area that will be under stress, such as on a fitted pants crotch or an underarm seam, it may be necessary to reinforce the seamline. After serge-seaming the garment, straight-stitch along the needleline on the crotch curve or underarm seamline between the notches. (Fig. 3-30)

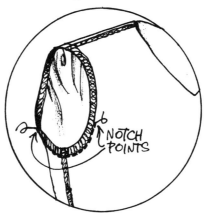

Fig. 3-30 Reinforce stress areas by straight-stitching on the serged needleline.

If you are serge-seaming with a stretchier 3- or 3/4-thread stitch, some areas, such as waistlines and necklines, may need to be reinforced. Serge over a lightweight stabilizer such a bias tricot strip (*Seams Great*, for example), a strip of fusible knit interfacing, or clear polyurethane elastic. Measure and cut the stabilizer using the pattern, rather than the garment, in case the fabric has already stretched a little. Place the fabric right sides together and put the stabilizer strip over the

seamline. Serge-seam through all layers with the needle on the seamline. (Fig. 3-31)

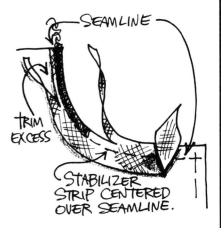

Fig. 3-31 To stabilize an edge, serge over bias tricot, fusible knit, or clear elastic.

When stabilizing a neckline edge, test first to be sure the garment will fit easily over your head after it is seamed.

To stabilize a shoulder seam, serge-finish the edges of the 5/8" seam allowances and straight-stitch the seam. Press the allowances open and top-stitch 1/4" on each side of the seamline. (Fig. 3-32) If you are plan-

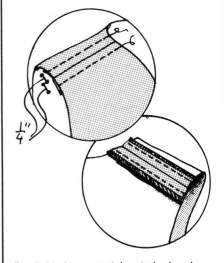

Fig. 3-32 Use a straight-stitched and top-stitched seam to stabilize the shoulder area.

ning to attach shoulder pads with *Velcro*, center a 3" *Velcro* strip (the soft side) under the seam before top-stitching. To omit the top-stitched effect and still reinforce the seam, simply stitch-in-the-ditch to attach the strip.

Negotiating Corners and Curves

One of the earliest lessons you probably learned on your serger was how to serge curves and corners. If you have not had much experience, practice before tackling them on a garment project. For detailed instructions, refer to a beginning serging book such as *ABCs of Serging* (listed under "Other Books by the Authors" at the back of this book).

Outside corners—The easiest method of serging an outside corner is to serge off one edge, turn the fabric, and serge back onto the adjoining edge.

Serging off and on a corner on some lightweight, slippery, or loosely woven fabrics, especially when using a rolled edge, may not give you a perfect right angle and thus may look "home-sewn." Perfect the corner by using water-soluble stabilizer:

1. Serge-seam or serge-finish one side using a rolled edge and chaining off at the corner.

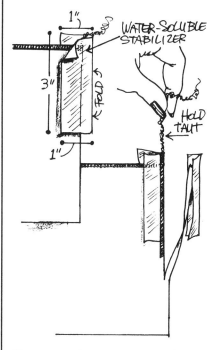

Fig. 3-33 Perfect square corners by serging the second side over water-soluble stabilizer.

2. Fold a 2" by 3" piece of water-soluble stabilizer over the corner. (Fig. 3-33)

3. Leaving a 2" to 3" thread chain, serge onto the unfinished corner, holding the thread chain taut.

If your fabric is washable, rinse away the stabilizer. The residue that remains will cause the corners to be slightly stiffer than the rest of the serged edge and will reinforce them. For dry-clean-only fabric, simply tear away the stabilizer.

On a small project, such as a scarf, collar, or belt, quickly dry the corners by using a hair dryer or heating them in a microwave oven. Set the timer on one-minute increments until the fabric is dry. Remember not to put any metallic fabric or thread in the microwave.

4. Tear away the stabilizer, dab the corners with seam sealant, and trim the thread chain when dry.

Inside corners—Inside corners or angles are easier to serge if you think of them as serging in a straight line. Simply pull the fabric out straight in front of the presser foot before it reaches the knives.

To be sure the serging catches all the fabric at a corner point, especially when serging a slit, gently push the fabric toward the needle. (Fig. 3-34)

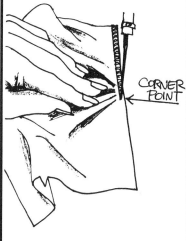

Fig. 3-34 Push the fabric toward the needle so the stitches catch the edge evenly.

Curves—When serging a curve, always guide the fabric in front of the presser foot as if you were serging a straight seam. Some tips:

✄ For an outside curve, when you pull the fabric out straight in front of the needle, you'll be moving the fabric to the right. For an inside curve, you'll move the fabric to the left. (Fig. 3-35)

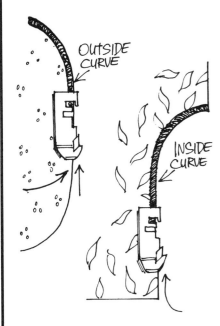

Fig. 3-35 Guide the fabric on any curve so that it feeds straight under the presser foot.

✄ Watch the knives or the needleline marking on the front of the presser foot instead of the needle.

> If you haven't done so already, mark the needleline position on the front of your presser foot using a fine-tipped permanent marker. For easy accuracy, guide the stitching line under the foot at the marking.

✄ Serge slowly around curves for the best stitch quality.

✄ If stitches bunch up as you serge around a curve, narrow the stitch width.

✄ Use the differential feed at 2.0 or ease-plus (see Fig. 3-6) to prevent stretching while serging a curve on less stable fabric.

✄ When serging in a circle, end by overlapping the stitching approximately 1/2", being careful not to cut the beginning stitches.

Serging Darts

Your serger can be used to seam darts quickly, but remember that the dart fabric will be trimmed away by the serging so alterations and adjustments won't be possible.

To make a dart, fold the fabric right sides together on the center line, matching the stitching lines and dots. Serge-seam, beginning at the widest part with the needle on the stitching line. Serge off at the point, leaving a 3" thread chain. Knot the chain at the fabric edge to secure. (Fig. 3-36)

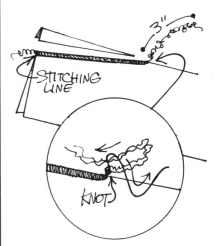

Fig. 3-36 Quickly serge-seam a dart and knot the thread chain at the point.

> Quickly mark a dart stitching line by placing transparent tape just to the left of the line.

Fast Interfacing Techniques

Method 1—For less show-through, apply interfacing to a facing rather than to the garment fabric, especially when using fusible interfacing. Finish facings by fusing interfacing to each piece. Then straight-stitch the interfaced facings together and press the seams open for the flattest application. For a neat, professional finish, serge-finish around the outside facing edge, trimming 1/4". (Fig. 3-37)

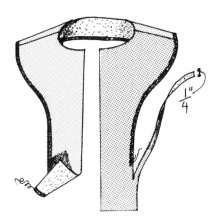

Fig. 3-37. Clean-finish by serging around the outside edges of the interfaced facings.

Method 2—To hide the serging on the inside of the garment, face the facing with either fusible or sew-in interfacing. Cut the interfacing using the garment facing pieces and do not trim.

1. Straight-stitch the facings together and press the allowances open. Repeat stitching for the interfacing sections, except serge-seam instead of straight-stitching. Do not press fusible interfacing.

2. With the facings and inter-facings right sides together, serge-seam the outer edges using a medium-length, medium-width, balanced 3-thread stitch. (Fig. 3-38)

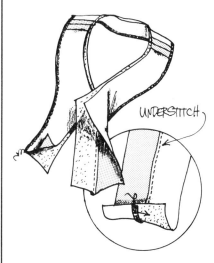

UNDERSTITCH

Fig. 3-38 To hide the serged stitching, face the facings before applying.

3. Finger-press the allowance toward the interfacing and understitch from the right side of the interfacing.

4. When using fusible interfacing, carefully press-baste the interfacing to the facing with wrong sides together. Then permanently fuse it in place. (With sew-in interfacing, carefully press.) Glue-stick or machine-baste the remaining seam allowances together before seaming the facing to the garment.

> If you must fuse interfacing to the garment front, interface the entire front. When interfacing the back (as for jackets), use pinking shears to cut the outer unseamed edge of the interfacing so it is less likely to show from the right side.

When using fusible knit interfacing on knit fabric, cut with the stretch going the same direction as the fabric, except when stabilization is needed. To stabilize buttonholes, cut the interfacing with the stretch going in the direction opposite the buttonholes. (Fig. 3-39)

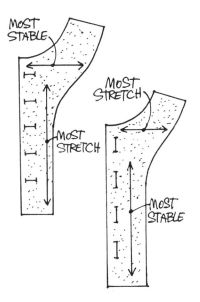

MOST STABLE
MOST STRETCH
MOST STRETCH
MOST STABLE

Fig. 3-39 Cut fusible knit interfacing with the most stretch perpendicular to the buttonholes.

NOTES

SERGED NECKLINE FINISHES

Serged Neckline Finishes

Serged Necklines ✄ Faced Necklines ✄ Ribbed Finishes ✄ Bound Necklines ✄ Banded Necklines
Keyhole Openings ✄ Speedy Serged Placket ✄ Collar Application ✄ Blouse and Jacket Techniques

The neckline is often the focal point of a garment, so it must be finished neatly and professionally. To do this, more time and care than are usually required for the rest of the garment may be necessary. For more accuracy, you'll usually want to finish the neckline before the rest of the garment is constructed. First seam one or both of the shoulders and apply the neckline either flat or in a circle, depending on the technique you are using and the desired finished appearance.

To finish any neckline opening, follow these simple guidelines:

✄ Because of the curved edges, a neckline opening can be stretched out of shape easily, so some kind of stabilization is necessary.

✄ When finishing a round neckline without a placket opening, try on the garment first to make sure it will fit over your head. To enlarge the opening,

trim from the center front to the shoulder seams 1/4" at a time (see Fig. 1-9).

✄ The center front of a jewel neckline should be at least 2" lower than the center back.

✄ When applying any serged neckline, it is easier and more accurate to serge with narrower seam allowances. Before serging, trim any 5/8" allowances to 1/4". Then skim the edge slightly with the knives when serge-seaming so the needle is directly on the seamline.

✄ Measure carefully when cutting and finishing a V-neckline. You may choose to alter a rounded jewel neckline to form a V. First, decide how you will finish the neckline before cutting. Then measure the desired depth of the finished V-opening from the upper center-front edge, as follows:

• *When binding the edge*, the neckline opening will finish at the cut edge of the opening.

• *When finishing the neckline by adding a self-fabric or ribbed band*, the trim will bring the finished neckline higher— the width of the finished band or ribbing minus the seam-allowance width.

An easy and fast approach is to seam one shoulder, finish a circular or V-neckline flat, and then seam the second shoulder. This flat application works well when you are unsure of the neckline size and may need to make adjustments or when using a binding strip (accurate measuring and quartermarking prior to attachment are not required with the flat method).

On some neckline styles, the results of the flat application method may not be as smooth or bulk-free as desired, and the seam allowance of the second shoulder seam may be visible at the neckline edge. In that case, complete both shoulder seams and apply the neckline in a continuous circle for the neatest and most professional finish. (Fig. 4-1)

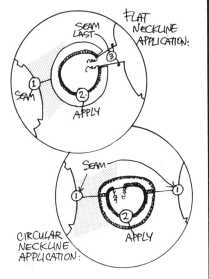

Fig. 4-1 Apply a neckline flat for speed and ease of handling. Apply it in a circle for a flatter, more finished neckline edge.

• *When facing the neckline,* the opening will be a seam-allowance width lower than the cut edge. (Fig. 4-2)

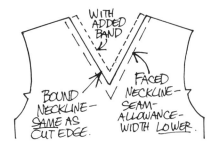

Fig. 4-2 Determine how you'll finish the neckline before deciding how deep to cut it.

If you are unsure about cutting the neckline, cut it an inch higher than calculated. After seaming the shoulder(s), fit the opening over your head. Using the previous guidelines, check to see that the finished neckline depth will be satisfactory.

Serged Necklines

The serger can neatly finish a neckline edge, but for durability the edge must be stabilized in some way—either by serging the edge over stabilizer or by turning the edge and top-stitching.

Decoratively serge-finished

Much of the fabric edge in a rounded neckline is on the bias grain so it has a tendency to stretch. In most cases, simply serge-finishing does not provide enough durability, so stabilization is necessary. During the application, you'll stay-stitch the neckline on the seamline using a short stitch length to prevent stretching and to make an accurate guide-line for the decorative stitching. First, remember to check the fit of the neckline opening.

Over filler cord—For a delicate neckline edge that will not receive excessive stress, decoratively serging over filler cord is an attractive finish:

1. Seam one shoulder and stay-stitch the neckline.

2. Adjust for a narrow, balanced 3-thread stitch or a rolled edge. Place filler cord (one or more strands of crochet thread or pearl cotton) under the back and over the front of the presser foot between the needle and the knives (or thread the filler through a specialty foot if one is available for your model). (Fig. 4-3) Serge over the filler for a few stitches before inserting the fabric under the foot.

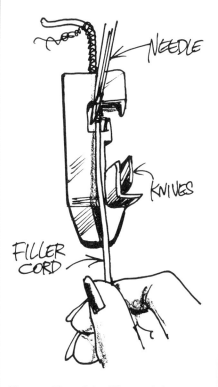

Fig. 4-3 Thread the filler cord through the foot and begin serging over it.

3. Serge-finish the right side of the neckline edge over the filler with the needle on the seamline. Be careful not to cut or stitch through the filler.

4. Seam the other shoulder by straight-stitching, back-stitching over the filler-cord ends to secure. Serge directly over the seamline or serge-finish the allowances together. (Fig. 4-4)

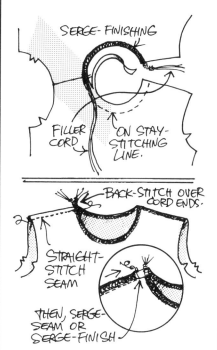

Fig. 4-4 Stabilize by decoratively serging over filler cord.

Over fabric selvage or narrow stay tape—When you want a little more stability but not the bulk of a facing or binding, decoratively serge over a strip of fabric selvage, stable lining fabric, or narrow stay tape to provide durability.

1. Cut a strip of garment fabric selvage (excellent for sheers) or another stay strip the length of the neckline plus 2".

2. Seam both shoulders.

3. Place the stabilizer over the wrong side of the neckline seamline, overlapping the ends at one shoulder seam. Stay-stitch the neckline through the stabilizer.

4. Trim the stay strip close to the stitching to the left of the seamline (on the garment side).

5. Starting at one shoulder seam and from the right side, serge-finish the neckline edge with the needle on the seamline. Use a rolled edge or narrow balanced stitch, overlapping the stitching ends for 1/2". (Fig. 4-5)

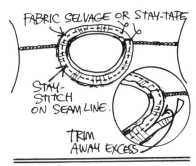

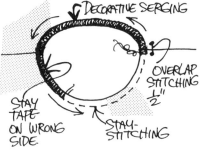

Fig. 4-5 Stabilize by serge-finishing over a neckline stay.

Serge-finish over a strip of bias tricot or 3/8"-wide clear elastic, following the previous instructions, for a stretchable but stabilizing finish.

Serged, turned, and top-stitched

Serge-finishing and top-stitching is another fast and easy method to neatly finish a round neckline. This technique also omits a bulkier facing and more stabilizing binding, but it is usually more stable than merely serge-finishing the neckline edge.

The fabric and neckline shape will dictate whether or not to use this finish—it works especially well for knits and more gentle curves. If the curves do not turn easily, use a narrower seam allowance.

1. Seam one shoulder.

2. Serge-finish the neckline edge using a medium-width, medium-length, balanced stitch.

3. Seam the other shoulder.

4. Turn 1/4" to 1/2" to the wrong side and top-stitch using straight-stitching, a twin-needle,

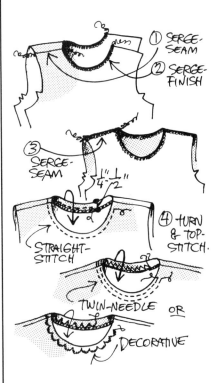

Fig. 4-6 Serge-finish, turn, and top-stitch for a quick and easy neckline treatment.

or an optional decorative stitch on the sewing machine. (Fig. 4-6)

> To prevent thread breakage when using a single needle to top-stitch a neckline edge that has any stretch or give, stretch the fabric slightly while stitching.

For an ornamental effect, serge-finish from the wrong side using decorative thread. Turn the finished allowance to the right side and top-stitch it in place.

Decoratively self-bound

On a stretchy, softly curved knit neckline, the edge can be attractively self-bound to create a beefier finish with added stability. Because it is so stable, be sure to check that the finished opening will fit over your head.

1. Cut the neckline with a 7/8" seam allowance.

2. Seam the shoulders.

3. Thread the upper looper with decorative thread and adjust for the widest balanced 3-thread stitch in any desired length.

> For a smooth, satin-length finish, use a short stitch but be sure the density of the stitches does not ruffle the edge.

4. Serge-finish the neckline edge from the wrong side without trimming.

5. Fold the serged-finished edge 7/8" to the wrong side and serge the fold.

6. Wrap the edge serged in step 4 to the right side and top-stitch it in place. (Fig. 4-7)

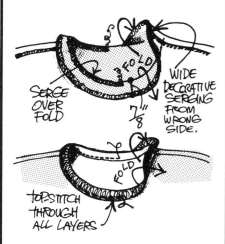

Fig. 4-7 A decorative self-binding can be used on a stretchable knit neckline.

Faced Necklines

Facings are often more bulky than other neckline techniques but they provide a neat, professional finish. For less bulk, consider facing with a lighter-weight fabric. Use a contrasting color or textured fabric for decorative detailing.

Round neckline facing

1. Interface the facing using the techniques outlined on page 33.

2. Seam the front and back neckline facings together. Straight-stitch and press the seams open for the flattest seaming. If you choose to serge-seam, press the allowance in the direction opposite the shoulder seam allowance for less bulk.

3. After seaming the garment shoulders, place the facing and garment necklines right sides together and serge-seam. (Fig. 4-8)

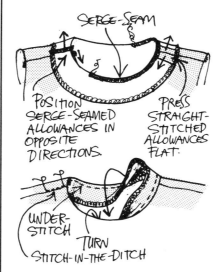

Fig. 4-8 Face a round neckline for a professional-looking finish.

After serge-seaming the neckline, there is no need to trim or clip as you would when sewing conventionally. Use the widest stitch except for very curved areas or a V-neck; then a medium stitch width is best.

4. Press the seam allowance toward the facing and understitch.

5. Press the facing to the inside of the garment and stitch-in-the-ditch of the shoulder seams to secure.

When facing a round neckline with a back zipper opening, wrap the facing ends around the back seamline above the zipper. Serge-seam through all layers. Then turn the facing to the wrong side and hand-tack the edges in place. (Fig. 4-9)

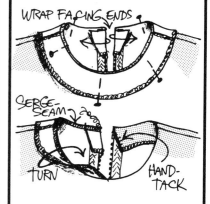

Fig. 4-9 Apply a facing over a zipper by wrapping the ends before serge-seaming.

Add a decorative finish to the garment by applying the facing to the outside of the neckline. When seaming, place the right side of the facing against the wrong side of the neckline. Omit the under-stitching but edge-stitch along the neckline if desired. Finish the exposed facing in one of two ways:

✂ Decoratively serge-finish the facing edges from the right side first and, after applying, top-stitch close to the overlocked edge to secure. (Fig. 4-10)

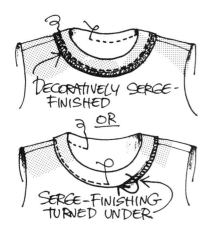

Fig. 4-10 Top-stitch the facing to the right side of the neckline for a decorative effect.

✂ Serge-finish the facing edge and turn it to the wrong side, using the serged stitch as a guide. After applying, top-stitch next to the fold to secure the facing edge.

> **When serge-finishing the outside curved edge prior to turning it under, adjust the differential feed to 2.0 or ease-plus manually to help ease the edge when turning.**

Doubled facing

Apply a durable doubled facing on gauze or other lightweight fabrics, even if the pattern does not include a facing.

1. Trim the garment neckline seam allowances to 1/4". Seam the garment shoulders.

2. Cut 1"-wide neckline facings using the pattern's new front and back neckline as a guide. Interface the facings and seam them together as in the previous step 2 on page 39. Serge-finish the outside facing edge.

3. With wrong sides together, serge-seam the facing to the neckline edge, using the widest balanced stitch.

4. Fold 3/8" of the facing toward the garment wrong side and top-stitch 1/4" from the fold, using straight-stitching or a twin-needle. Steam and finger-press the edge flat. (Fig. 4-11)

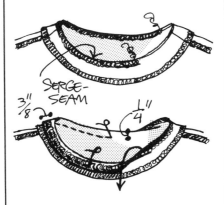

Fig. 4-11 Apply a doubled facing for extra stability.

Reversed narrow facing

Use a doubled strip as a narrow facing on the right side of a T-shirt or other casual garment.

1. Cut the strip 1-1/2" wide. On knits, position the greatest stretch lengthwise. For wovens, use a bias strip.

2. Fold the strip in half lengthwise, wrong sides together, and serge-seam it to the wrong side of the garment edge. (Fig. 4-12)

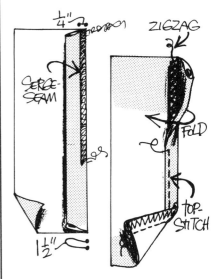

Fig. 4-12 Neatly finish a knit neckline with a reversed narrow facing.

3. Zigzag the seam allowance to the garment.

4. Fold the strip to the right side, covering the seam allowance, and top-stitch it in place.

V-neckline facing

A faced V-neckline may also be serge-seamed, although the V will be slightly more rounded than when done by conventional methods. Seam both garment shoulders, as well as the facing shoulders.

1. Before serging the neckline, mark the seamline of the V by stay-stitching on the seamline for 2" on each side of the point. (Fig. 4-13)

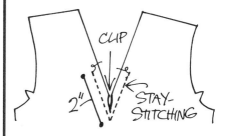

Fig. 4-13 Clip the neckline point to within 1/8" of the stay-stitching.

2. Clip to within 1/8" of the stay-stitching at the V.

3. Place the facing on the garment, right sides together. Work with the garment side on top. Beginning at one shoulder seam, serge-seam, pulling the fabric straight at the V, as described on page 31, and finish by overlapping the stitching ends. Position the needle on the stay-stitching line as you serge the point of the V. (Fig. 4-14)

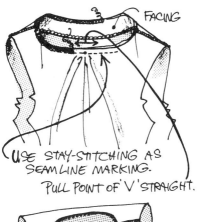

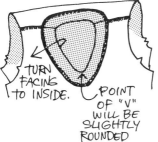

Fig. 4-14 Serge-seam the facing to the V-neckline in a circle.

Ribbed Finishes

Ribbing is another easy serged option for finishing a neckline. You can quickly and professionally serge-seam any width ribbed band to the neckline of a woven or knit garment. A knit self-fabric band may be used in place of ribbing with some length alterations (see the chart on page 42). Follow these simple tips for serging ribbing:

✄ With few exceptions, cut the ribbing smaller than the neckline opening and stretch it to fit during application so it will hug the neck.

✄ Ribbing varies in stretch and recovery, so test by fitting the fabric around your head before cutting.

✄ Before applying, trim any 5/8" seam allowances on the ribbed band and the neckline to 1/4" for the easiest and most accurate application.

✄ Cut the ribbing with the greatest stretch going the length of the ribbed band.

✄ When seaming ribbing in a circle, straight-stitch and finger-press open the seam for the flattest option.

✄ Serge-seam ribbing with a long, wide, balanced stitch to avoid stretching it. Adjust the differential feed to 2.0 to help ease the garment fabric to the ribbing. Press only the seam allowances of the ribbing, not its body, to avoid stretching it out of shape.

Ribbing Guidelines

Neckline	Trim Out Opening	Length of Band	Width of Band
Crew	3/4" from neckline for 1-1/4" finished band on knits; 1" or more from neckline for woven fabrics	2/3 neckline measurement for ribbing; 3/4 neckline measurement for self-fabric	3" for 1-1/4" finished band
Mock turtleneck	3/4" from neckline for knits; 1" or more for wovens	2/3 neckline measurement for ribbing; 3/4 neckline measurement for self-fabric	5"
Turtleneck	No trimming (usually used only on knits without an opening)	Same as neckline	11"
Cowl	Cut front neckline 1" lower, tapering to shoulder	Same as neckline	15"
V-neck	3/4" from back neckline; 7" to 8" from center front, tapering to 3/4" at shoulders	Same as neckline	3" for 1-1/4" finished band

✂ When serge-seaming most applications, sew with the ribbing on top.

✂ As you stretch the ribbing to fit the neckline, stretch more around curves and less on straight edges.

Patterns that call for ribbing measure it either by length or by using a guide. But, following a few simple guidelines, you can add ribbing to any basic jewel neckline whether or not the pattern calls for it. To determine the ribbing length, measure the seamline at the neckline opening. Test to be sure the ribbing and garment opening will fit comfortably over your head before applying the ribbing, and trim the neckline seam allowance to 1/4".

Round ribbed necklines

Ribbing may be applied flat or in a circle. The flat application is faster but the circular application finishes the neckline edge neatly with no visible seam allowances (see Fig. 4-1).

Flat ribbing application:

1. Seam one shoulder.

2. Fold the band in half lengthwise with wrong sides together and serge-seam it to the neckline using a long, wide, balanced stitch. Stretch gently around the curves.

3. Finger-press the seam allowance toward the garment. To add durability and a crisper finish, you may choose to top-stitch from the right side using straight-stitching or a twin-needle, catching the seam allowance.

4. Matching the ribbing seam-lines, seam the other shoulder through the band. (Fig. 4-15)

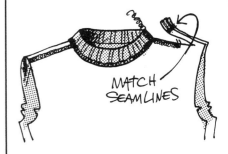

Fig. 4-15 Check to be sure the ribbing band is long enough to fit over your head.

Fashionably finish a lower, scooped neckline with a narrower ribbed band. Cut ribbing or knit self-fabric the length of the neckline seamline by 1-1/2" for a 1/2"-wide band. (When using a striped knit fabric for the band, you may want to cut it on the bias for a decorative effect.) Apply the ribbing following the previous instructions, stretching gently around the curves and firmly at the center front. Finger-press the seam allowance toward the garment and top-stitch through all layers from the right side, 1/8" from the seamline, before completing the second shoulder seam. (Fig. 4-16)

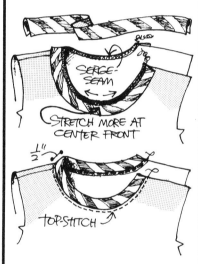

Fig. 4-16 Apply a narrower, 1-1/2"-wide knit strip to a scoop neckline for a 1/2"-wide band.

Circular ribbing application:

1. Seam the short ends of the ribbing to form a circle. Finger-press the seam open.

2. Fold the circle in half lengthwise with wrong sides together.

3. Quartermark the ribbing and the neckline opening by folding in fourths and marking with pins, placing the seam at one quartermark.

The ribbing seam should be placed at the center back during application. The shoulder seams are usually not halfway between center front and center back so they will not be at the quartermarks. (Fig. 4-17)

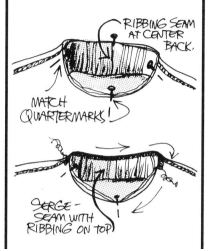

Fig. 4-17 Apply circular ribbing by quartermarking the folded ribbed band and the neckline edge. Serge-seam through all layers.

4. Matching the quartermarks, serge-seam the ribbing to the opening, removing the pins before they reach the knives.

5. Carefully press the seam allowance toward the garment and, if desired, top-stitch as in step 3 of the instructions given previously for flat ribbing application.

Ribbed V-neckline

Ribbing is most easily applied to a V-neckline using the flat method.

1. Stay-stitch the seamline 2" on either side of the V and clip to within 1/8" of the point. (See Fig. 4-13)

2. Seam one shoulder.

3. Fold the ribbing in half lengthwise with wrong sides together. Serge-seam the ribbing to the garment with the garment on top, pulling the edge straight at the point of the V and stretching the ribbing across the back neckline. (Fig. 4-18)

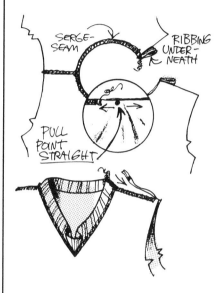

Fig. 4-18 Serge-seam the folded ribbing to the neckline edge, then seam the second shoulder.

4. Seam the other shoulder through the ribbing.

5. Fold the front right sides together and straight-stitch the ribbing along the center-front line. (Fig. 4-19)

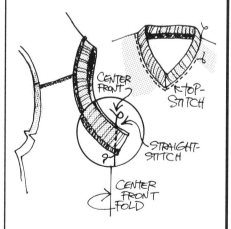

Fig. 4-19 Straight-stitch through the ribbing at the center front. Top-stitch the seam allowance to the garment.

6. From the wrong side, carefully press the ribbing flat at the center front. Finger-press the allowance toward the garment and top-stitch through all layers from the right side to secure.

> **When applying a wide V-neck ribbing, stitch-in-the-ditch of the vertical center-front seam to secure the pleat underneath. (Fig. 4-20)**
>
>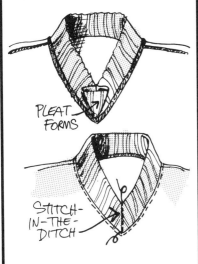
>
> Fig. 4-20 Stitch-in-the-ditch at the center front to stabilize the pleat underneath.

Ruffled ribbing

Lettuce the edge or center of a ribbed band to add a feminine effect. The band should be 1-1/4" or wider to ruffle the edge most easily. Use a 2-1/2" or wider band if ruffling the center.

1. Apply ribbing to a round neckline following the instructions given previously for circular ribbing.

2. Adjust your serger for a satin-length rolled-edge stitch.

3. Starting at the band center-back seamline, serge-finish the edge, stretching firmly while serging and being careful not to cut the fold. Overlap the stitching ends for 1/2". To lettuce the

center of the band, refold along the midpoint of the band front before serging. (Fig. 4-21)

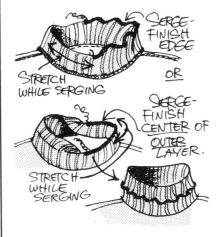

Fig. 4-21 Ruffle the ribbed band edge or refold to ruffle the center.

Sweater ribbing

Sweater ribbing is usually softer than T-shirt ribbing and frequently will have less recovery when stretched. Follow these simple guidelines when serging sweater ribbing:

✄ For easiest application and least stretching, cut a wide ribbing strip (plan for at least a 1-1/4" or wider finished width).

✄ Always serge-seam using the longest, widest balanced stitch.

✄ Apply sweater ribbing with the ribbing on top (similar to the previous ribbing application instructions). But in this case, don't stretch the ribbing to fit the neckline edge. Instead, ease the sweatering underneath to fit the unstretched ribbing. This prevents the ribbing from stretching permanently out of shape. Adjust the differential feed to 2.0 so the machine can help with the easing.

✄ Steam and finger-press the seam allowances only, without touching the iron to the fabric. Allow the fabric to cool completely before moving it.

For the flattest, least bulky application, attach ribbing single layer, folding over the opposite edge to imitate knitted-on sweater ribbing. Use this technique on sweater necklines or for any other ribbed band application. (Fig. 4-22)

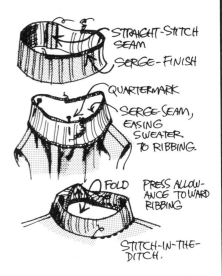

Fig. 4-22 Apply sweater ribbing single layer for the flattest finish.

1. Seam the shoulders.

2. Cut the ribbing according to the pattern instructions or the chart on page 42.

> **Because you've trimmed your garment's seam allowances to 1/4", if pattern instructions call for 5/8" seam allowances on the ribbing band, cut 1/4" allowances on the band instead.**

3. Serge-finish one long edge of the ribbing without easing or stretching it.

4. Straight-stitch the strip into a circle and finger-press the seam allowances open.

5. Trim the neckline seam allowances to 1/4" if they are wider. Quartermark the ribbing circle and the neckline opening. With right sides together, pin the single-layer unserged ribbing edge to the neckline, matching the quartermarks.

6. Serge-seam, easing the sweater to the ribbing.

> **When using this technique for a T-shirt or other nonsweater garment, stretch the ribbing to fit the neckline edge.**

7. Steam only the seam allowance and finger-press it toward the ribbing.

8. Fold the serge-finished edge over the seam, matching the needlelines. Stitch-in-the-ditch from the right side to secure.

Bound Necklines

When a facing would be too bulky or would show through to the right side, binding the neckline edge is a fast and durable option. (Fig. 4-23) Use it if appropriate ribbing is not available and the neckline needs more stabilization than a turned and top-stitched finish. Binding can be used for any neckline shape and is applied using the flat order of construction.

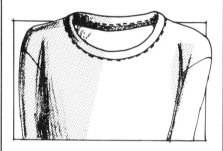

Fig. 4-23 Binding stabilizes a neckline edge quickly and easily.

Follow these easy guidelines:

✄ Because the cut edge will be equal to the edge of the finished neckline, trim away the neckline seam allowances before applying the binding.

✄ When binding a round neckline, first be sure the opening is large enough to fit over your head. Woven fabrics will require a larger opening than stretchable knits.

✄ Use matching or contrasting fabric for the binding strip. Ribbing also works well. Cut a woven strip on the bias and a knit strip with the greatest stretch running lengthwise.

✄ Cut the binding strip the length of the opening plus 2".

✄ The finished binding width is determined by the width of the seam used to apply it to the neckline. When serge-seaming, the finished binding width is the width of the serged seam allowance. If you prefer a wider binding, straight-stitch the seam. Seam widths of 5/8" or less work best for a bound neckline.

> **When binding medium- to heavy-weight fabric, the bulk of the fabric may make the finished binding up to 1/4" wider than the seam. Be sure to test first and allow extra width, if necessary, when cutting the binding strip.**
>
> **If you choose to straight-stitch the binding to the neckline, serge-finish the seam allowances together for easier wrapping.**

✄ Cut the strip width three times the finished stitch width plus 1/4" for light- to medium-weight fabrics or four times the stitch width plus 1/4" for heavy or bulky fabrics. If you will serge-seam the neckline binding, cut the strip 1" wide (three times a 1/4" seam allowance width plus 1/4").

✄ When applying the binding, stretch slightly around the curved areas so the binding will lay flat against the neck.

✄ For the flattest binding application, construct the garment by serge-finishing, straight-stitching, and pressing the seams open—especially the last shoulder seam.

Binding application

1. Trim off the neckline seam allowances.

2. Cut a binding strip as described previously and serge-finish one long edge.

3. Seam one shoulder, right sides together. Press the seam open.

4. Right sides together, seam the binding strip to the neckline by serging or straight-stitching. If serging, just skim the edges with the knives and do not trim. (Fig. 4-24)

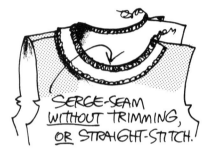

Fig. 4-24 Seam the binding strip to the neckline edge.

At this point, pin the remaining shoulder seam through the bound neckline edge. Fit the opening over your head. If it is too tight, remove the binding and re-seam. The binding can tighten up the opening if it is stretched significantly during application. Stretching less on the curves may be all that is needed to perfect the fit. If you are unsure about the size of the neckline when cutting out the garment, however, cut the binding strip several inches longer than the opening in case the neckline needs to be lowered.

5. Press both the binding and the seam allowance away from the garment. Matching the binding seamline with right sides together, seam the second shoulder including the binding.

6. Wrap the binding tightly around the seam allowance and secure by one of the following methods:

• Stitch-in-the-ditch from the right side.

• Top-stitch on the binding strip next to the seamline, using straight-stitching, a twin-needle stitch, or a decorative sewing-machine stitch. (Fig. 4-25)

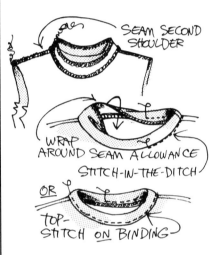

Fig. 4-25 Seam the second shoulder before wrapping and stitching to secure the binding.

If you prefer the binding to be finished on the inside, cut the strip 1/4" wider. After wrapping, turn the serge-finished edge to the wrong side and secure it by one of the methods outlined previously. Use the serge-finishing as a guide for easy turning. (Fig. 4-26)

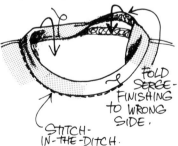

Fig. 4-26 Clean-finish the inside neckline by cutting a wider binding strip and folding the edge under before wrapping.

To add a self-fabric or lace ruffle to a bound neckline edge, place the wrong side of the ruffle against the right side of the neckline. With a medium-length balanced stitch, serge-baste the edges together. Bind the neckline through both the ruffle and the garment, following the previous page instructions and cutting a slightly wider binding strip to allow for the bulk of the gathered edge. (Fig. 4-27)

Fig. 4-27 Apply binding over the ruffle edge and the neckline edge simultaneously.

Banded Necklines

Self-fabric or contrasting bands can neatly finish a neckline edge and add stability. Banded necklines are usually constructed using the flat order of construction. Cut a woven fabric band on the bias and a knit band in the direction of greatest stretch. Consider using woven bands on knits for stabilization and decorative contrast. Vary the band width if desired—a narrow band gives the appearance of piping but it is much faster and easier to apply than piping.

Band application

1. For a 1/2" finished band, cut a strip 1-1/2" wide by the length of the neckline opening plus 1".

2. Seam one shoulder.

> **Pin the other shoulder seam and fit the neckline over your head before applying the band. If necessary, trim out the front neckline edge to make a larger opening, following the instructions on page 5.**

3. Fold the band in half lengthwise with wrong sides together. Serge the band to the right side of the neckline opening, matching the cut edges. Stretch slightly around the curves so the finished band will lay smoothly against the neck. (Fig. 4-28)

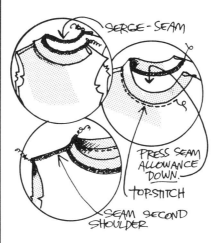

Fig. 4-28 Serge a fabric band onto the garment for a simple neckline finish.

4. Press the seam allowance toward the garment. From the right side, top-stitch 1/8" from the seamline through all layers to secure the allowance.

5. Matching the band seamlines, seam the other shoulder including the band. Top-stitch to secure the seam allowance as shown in Fig. 1-11.

> **When applying a 1-1/4"-wide band to a jacket or cardigan neckline, cut a strip 3" wide by the length of the neckline edge plus 1". Seam both shoulders and apply the band as previously described. Gently stretch the band around the curves but not on the straight edges.**

Banded V-neck

Adding a band to a V-neckline is most easily done when the garment has a center-front seam with 5/8" seam allowances—add them to the pattern if necessary.

1. Cut the band the length of the finished neckline plus 2". Serge-finish (but don't seam) the center-front seam allowances and seam the shoulders.

2. Using the widest balanced stitch, serge-seam the band to the neckline with at least 1" of the band extending on each end. (Fig. 4-29)

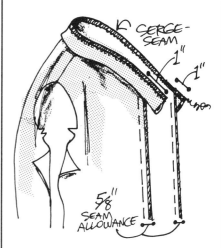

Fig. 4-29 Apply a band to a V-neckline before seaming the center front.

3. Finger-press the seam allowance toward the garment.

4. With right sides together, match the seam allowance and the band. Straight-stitch the center-front seam, extending through the band. Press the seam open and serge-seam the ends to the allowances underneath. (Fig. 4-30)

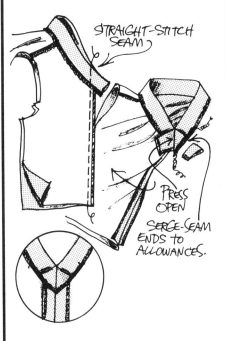

Fig. 4-30 After seaming the center front, press the ends open and serge-seam them to the allowances underneath, trimming off the excess.

5. Top-stitch next to the seamline from the right side to secure the neckline seam allowance.

Keyhole Openings

Keyhole openings may be serged with or without a center-back seam. Finish a seamed opening most quickly and neatly with your serger. Without a seam, the opening may also be finished using the serger, but a little more practice may be necessary to perfect the corner technique. Before finishing any keyhole opening, be sure the neckline will fit comfortably over your head. To make the opening larger, simply make the keyhole longer. Although keyholes are usually featured at the center back, you may use them elsewhere on the garment neckline or on a sleeve.

Keyhole with a seam

Finish a seamed keyhole opening using a separate facing or a cut-on facing.

With a separate facing:

1. Cut the center back seam with a 1" seam allowance. Using the neckline of the pattern, cut a neckline facing 2-1/2" wide (or the width of the front neckline facing if the pattern has one), eliminating the center-back seam allowance.

2. Separately seam the facing and bodice at the shoulders.

3. Serge-finish the outside facing edges and the garment center-back seam allowances.

4. Straight-stitch the center-back seam as far as the lower edge of the keyhole opening and back-stitch to secure. Press the seam open.

5. Place the facing on the neckline with right sides together. Fold the center-back seam allowances under the ends of the facing. (Fig. 4-31)

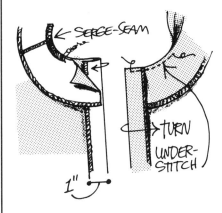

Fig. 4-31 Hide the ends of a separate facing under a wide seam allowance.

6. Serge-seam the neckline, press the seam allowance toward the facing, and under-stitch. Turn the facing and seam allowances to the wrong side, pressing carefully.

With a cut-on facing:

1. To alter the bodice back pattern, trace the back neckline facing and taper to a 1" seam allowance at the center-back opening. (Fig. 4-32)

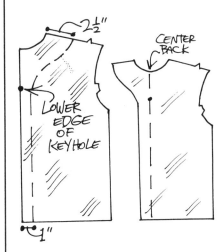

Fig. 4-32 Alter the bodice back pattern to include a cut-on keyhole facing.

2. Seam the shoulders of both the facing and the bodice.

3. Serge-finish the outer facing and seam-allowance edges.

4. With right sides together, straight-stitch the center-back seam up to the lower edge of the opening. Carefully press the allowances open.

5. With right sides together and cut edges matching, serge-seam the facing and bodice at the neckline. Under-stitch and turn the facing to the wrong side. (Fig. 4-33)

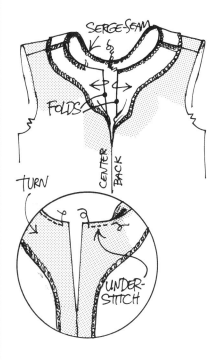

Fig. 4-33 Serge-seam the facing and bodice together at the neckline edge.

Keyhole without a seam

Several serger methods may be used to finish the keyhole opening when it is not on a seamline:

✄ Using a narrow rolled edge, decoratively serge-finish the slashed opening, pulling the point out in a straight line using the inside corner technique. (See Fig. 3-34)

✄ Bind the edge with a narrow binding:

1. Cut a narrow bias strip 1/2" wide by the length of the slit.

2. Using a narrow balanced stitch, serge-finish one long edge of the strip.

3. With right sides together and the garment on top, serge-seam the raw edge of the binding to the opening using the narrow balanced stitch.

4. Wrap the binding around the seam allowance to the wrong side and stitch-in-the-ditch to secure. (Fig. 4-34)

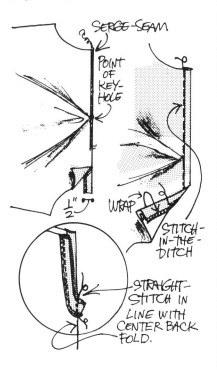

Fig. 4-34 Bind a keyhole with a narrow bias strip when it is not on a seamline.

5. With right sides together, fold and straight-stitch at the point of the opening.

✄ Serge-seam a facing to the opening:

1. Using the bodice pattern, draw and cut a back facing pattern 2-1/2" wide (or the width of the front facing if the pattern has one), tapering around the slit.

2. Serge-finish the outer facing edges.

3. With the garment and facing right sides together, cut the slash. Using a medium-width balanced stitch, serge-seam the opening, pulling the slit straight at the point.

4. Seam both the bodice and the facing at the shoulders. (Fig. 4-35)

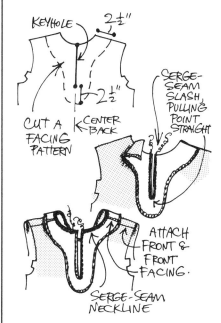

Fig. 4-35 A facing is another option for a keyhole not placed on a seamline.

5. With right sides together, serge-seam the neckline edge. Under-stitch and turn the facing to the inside, pressing the slit carefully. If desired, edge-stitch or top-stitch the neckline to finish.

Speedy Serged Placket

For a sporty neckline finish and a larger neckline opening, serge a placket on a basic pull-over or shell. Finish the neckline edge with serged binding (see page 45). For a 1"-wide finished placket:

1. Mark the center-front line with a crease or a water-soluble marker.

2. Measure the bodice front against your body to determine the desired length of the placket opening. From a piece of tear-away stabilizer, cut a stay 3" wide and 1" longer than the placket opening.

3. On the stay, mark a center-front line as shown in Fig. 4-36. Draw another line the finished length of the placket opening 1" to the left of the center-front line. Draw a stitching line 1/8" on either side of this opening line.

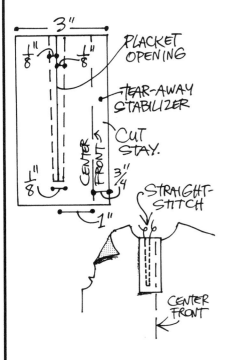

Fig. 4-36 Use a stay to make a speedy serged placket.

4. Pin the stay on the wrong side of the front, matching the center-front markings. Using a short stitch, straight-stitch through the stay and the garment on the stitching lines.

5. Cut on the opening line, being careful not to cut through the stitches. Remove the stay.

6. Cut a placket strip of woven or knit fabric, as shown in Fig. 4-37. Press the strip in half lengthwise with wrong sides together.

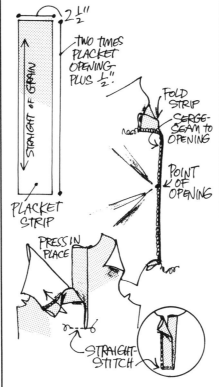

Fig. 4-37 Serge-seam a folded strip to the placket opening, press, and straight-stitch across the bottom.

7. Place the garment and placket right sides together and, with the wrong side of the garment on top, serge-seam, using a narrow balanced stitch, pulling the point out in a straight line following the inside corner technique (see page 31).

8. Carefully press the placket into position. From the right side of the garment, straight-stitch across the lower end of the placket through all layers, catching the placket fold in the stitching.

9. Seam the shoulders and bind the neckline, following the general instructions on page 46. Cut the binding strip the length of the neckline edge plus 1". To finish the ends when applying the binding, wrap 1/2" to the wrong side on each end before serge-seaming the neckline edge. Then wrap the binding to the wrong side and top-stitch. Add buttons or snaps, if desired. (Fig. 4-38)

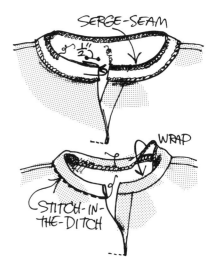

Fig. 4-38 Bind the neckline edge after applying the placket.

Collar Application

Serge-seam collars to eliminate the tedious trimming and clipping required for those sewn conventionally. Some tips:

✄ For the most stability and serging ease, interface an entire one-piece collar or both pieces of a two-piece collar. This will eliminate fabric slippage during serging and provide the neatest finish.

✄ Because the serger will trim away any notches, make all pattern markings on the seamline.

✄ Be sure to serge with the needle on the collar seamline so the collar will fit the neckline accurately.

Two-piece rectangular collars

On two-piece collars, trim 1/4" from the long outer edge of the undercollar before seaming, so the upper collar will roll to the underside.

1. Using a medium-length, medium-width, balanced 3-thread stitch, serge-seam the collar pieces, right sides together, on the long outer edge. (Fig. 4-39)

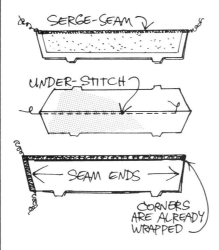

Fig. 4-39 For perfect rectangular collars, seam and under-stitch the outer edge to wrap the allowance toward the undercollar.

2. Press the collar flat and the seam allowance toward the undercollar. Under-stitch, helping to form perfect corners.

Intersecting serged seam allowances are usually too bulky to turn crisply and neatly at the collar points. To overcome this, complete the outer seam first and wrap the allowance toward the undercollar before serge-seaming the ends. The under-stitching does this automatically.

---

3. Carefully fold the collar with right sides together and serge-seam the collar ends. Secure the thread chain at the points. Turn the collar right side out and press again.

Rounded collars

Rounded collars may be serge-seamed without the concern of wrapping the corners as on rectangular collars. For the easiest construction:

✄ Test to be sure the serger will easily negotiate the curved edges. You may want to reshape to softer curves for more accurate stitching.

✄ Use a narrow, short to medium-length serged stitch for the easiest and most even serging.

✄ Stay-stitch the rounded seamlines to prevent stretching and to provide an accurate guideline for the serge-seaming.

Use a satin-length, rolled-edge stitch for a piped effect on the collar edge. Serge-seam the rounded collar with wrong sides together, using contrasting thread in the upper looper. The rolled-edge also can be used as a delicate seam on the inside of a sheer or lightweight rounded collar. (Fig. 4-40)

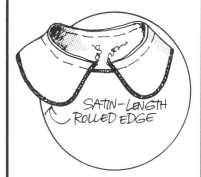

Fig. 4-40 For mock piping, seam lightweight fabric wrong sides together using a rolled-edge stitch.

For a feminine touch, construct a collar from lace yardage and serge-seam it to the neckline. Also consider using a purchased lace or finished knit collar on an appropriate garment. (Fig. 4-41)

Blouse and Jacket Techniques

Serge-seam to apply the collar and facing on most blouses and lightweight jackets. The serger eliminates the need to clip and trim the seam allowances and finishes the neckline edge neatly and professionally.

1. Seam the shoulders.

2. Place the finished collar on the neckline edge, with both right side up and the markings matched.

It is easier to serge the neckline if the seam allowances are narrow. Trim the neckline edge allowances of the collar, garment, and facing to 1/4".

3. Serge-finish the front facing on the outer and shoulder edges.

4. For a cut-on facing, fold right sides together, sandwiching the collar between. (Fig. 4-42)

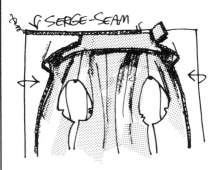

Fig. 4-42 Fold the facing over the collar before seaming the neckline through all layers.

Eliminate the back neckline facing on a blouse; it is not necessary to hide the neatly finished serged seamline. On a jacket, you may prefer to use a back neckline facing, attaching it to the front facing and serge-finishing the outer edge before folding it over the collar.

5. Serge-seam the neckline. Press the seam flat and then press it toward the garment. Fold the interfacing toward the inside. From the right side, top-stitch across the back through all layers between the shoulder seams.

If the facings are cut separately from the garment, attach them to the front edges. Then wrap the seam allowance back over the top of the facing before completing the neckline edge. This will wrap the front neckline corner points. (Fig. 4-43) After completing the neckline seam, turn the facings to the inside of the garment and press carefully.

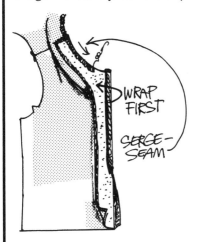

Fig. 4-43 For a perfect point at the neckline edge, wrap a facing seam toward the garment before serging the neckline.

SERGED FROM LACE FABRIC

PURCHASED KNIT COLLAR

PURCHASED LACE COLLAR

Fig. 4-41 Consider collar options other than self-fabric.

CHAPTER 5

SERGED SLEEVES

Serged Sleeves

Sleeve Application Methods

The method you choose for applying the sleeves to your garment will depend on the styling, the fabric, the amount of wear and tear you plan to give it, and your personal preference. When applying sleeves:

✄ Finish the lower sleeve edges flat, if possible, before seaming the sleeves and attaching them to the bodice.

✄ Check the fit and sleeve length before cutting out (see Chapter 2). This is especially important on fitted sleeves. Dropped shoulders and looser sleeves are more forgiving.

> If you're still unsure of the fit after the garment is cut out, baste the sleeves to the bodice first and try it on. Make adjustments, if necessary, before the final seaming.

Flat or shirt-style sleeve cap

This type of sleeve cap is featured in dropped-shoulder and more casual shirt styling. (Fig. 5-1) It is faster and easier to apply than a conventional set-in sleeve because it can be serged flat and requires little or no ease.

Fig. 5-1 Serge-seam a flat sleeve cap to the garment before completing the underarm seam.

1. If some easing of the sleeve cap is necessary before attaching it to the garment, adjust for a wide, medium-length, balanced 3- or 4-thread stitch.

> Because you will be trimming off any notches and matchpoints when you serge-finish the sleeve cap edge, transfer them first to a comparable point on the wrong side of the seamline. (Fig. 5-2)

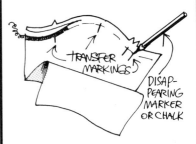

Fig. 5-2 Transfer markings to the seamline so they are visible after serge-easing.

2. Beginning at one edge, serge with the needle (left needle of a 4-thread stitch) just to the right of the seamline until you reach the first notch. Tighten the needle tension(s), lengthen the stitch, and increase the differential feed up to 2.0 (if available on your model) and serge the edge between the notches. (Fig. 5-3)

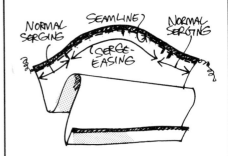

Fig. 5-3 Use a tighter needle tension, longer stitch, and differential feed to ease the sleeve cap between the notches.

3. After reaching the second notch, readjust to normal settings and finish serging to the end.

4. Trim the same amount off the armscye seam allowance as you trimmed off when serging the sleeve cap. Pin the sleeve to the armscye, right sides together, matching the markings and adjusting any fullness to fit.

Fig. 5-4 Create a little more easing by pulling the needle thread.

5. With the sleeve underneath (so the feed dogs will help ease any excess fabric), serge-seam the sleeve to the bodice.

6. Press the allowance toward the sleeve and, starting at the hem edge, serge-seam the garment and sleeve underarm. (Fig. 5-5)

PRESS ALLOWANCE

Fig. 5-5 Serge-seam the garment and sleeve underarm.

Full or high-cut sleeve cap

Used for a traditional set-in sleeve, this style is eased or gathered to the bodice during construction. (Fig. 5-6) If you need to ease or gather the sleeve cap significantly, if the armscye will receive a lot of stress (because of a close fit or constant wear), or if the fabric is loosely woven or difficult to handle, apply the sleeves conventionally and then serge-finish the allowances together. Most sewing professionals also prefer the more precise tailoring of a traditionally set-in sleeve on better fabrics.

Fig. 5-6 Gather a full sleeve cap and set in the sleeve conventionally.

1. Gather the sleeve cap using the serge-easing technique explained previously for a flat sleeve cap or machine-baste and ease conventionally. (Remember that the serge-eased sleeve will have a seam allowance only as wide as the serged stitch width.)

2. Complete the side seam and the sleeve underarm seam using the seaming method you have chosen for your garment.

3. Pin the sleeve to the bodice, right sides together, matching the pattern markings. Adjust the ease.

4. Straight-stitch the sleeve to the armscye along the seamline. If the sleeve cap has considerable gathering or if you are doing precise tailoring, sew with the sleeve on top to visually control the stitching. When sewing on a knit fabric or when excess gathers are not a problem, sew with the bodice on top so the feed dogs can help ease the sleeve fabric. (Fig. 5-7)

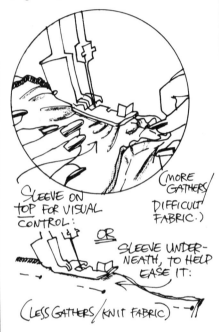

Fig. 5-7 Decide which side to seam from depending on the amount of gathering and the difficulty of easing the fabric.

5. Serge-finish the sleeve allowances together for a professional finish. The second row of stitching also adds durability to the seam.

When a set-in sleeve has minimal ease or if you are using a knit or stretch fabric, an acceptable option is to serge-seam instead of straight-stitching. Begin and end the serging just to the bodice back side of the underarm seam. Serge with the bodice on top so the machine can help ease in any fullness on the bottom layer. Straight-stitch along the needleline between the underarm notches to reinforce the stitching. (Fig. 5-8)

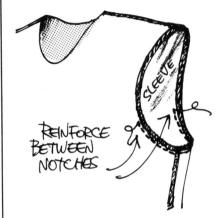

Fig. 5-8 Set in a sleeve using serge-seaming only when the fabric is stretchable or there is little ease.

Other sleeve types

Raglan sleeve—This sleeve style is easily applied by serge-seaming; however, any other seaming method described in Chapter 3 can be used. On a raglan sleeve, the top edge of the sleeve becomes part of the neckline edge. (Fig. 5-9)

Fig. 5-9 Apply a raglan sleeve using any seaming method.

> The prominent raglan-sleeve design lines are an excellent place to display decorative serging.

Dolman and kimono sleeves—Because they are cut onto the garment as an extension of the bodice, dolman and kimono sleeves don't need to be applied like other sleeve types. When serging the underarm seam on a kimono sleeve, reinforce the curved area using the techniques on page 30. A dolman sleeve underarm seam will often need reinforcement as well. (Fig. 5-10)

Fig. 5-10 When serge-seaming a cut-on sleeve, reinforce the underarm curves.

Sleeveless—The final sleeve option is to use no sleeves at all. Face or finish the armscye using any of the techniques discussed in Chapter 4 for finishing a round neckline.

BASIC PULLOVER TOP

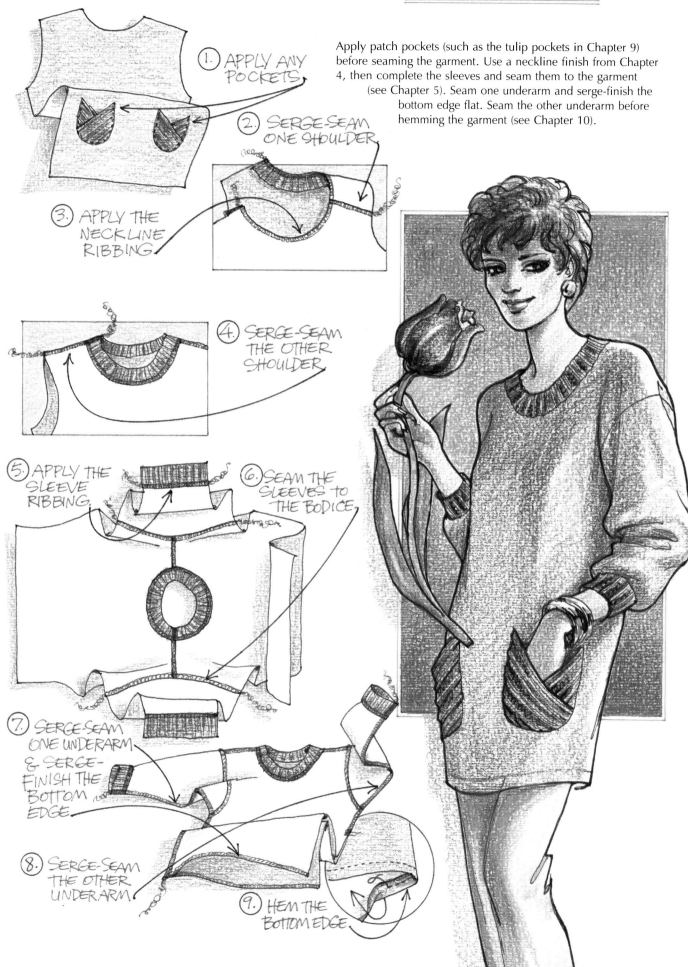

Apply patch pockets (such as the tulip pockets in Chapter 9) before seaming the garment. Use a neckline finish from Chapter 4, then complete the sleeves and seam them to the garment (see Chapter 5). Seam one underarm and serge-finish the bottom edge flat. Seam the other underarm before hemming the garment (see Chapter 10).

1. APPLY ANY POCKETS

2. SERGE-SEAM ONE SHOULDER

3. APPLY THE NECKLINE RIBBING

4. SERGE-SEAM THE OTHER SHOULDER

5. APPLY THE SLEEVE RIBBING

6. SEAM THE SLEEVES TO THE BODICE

7. SERGE-SEAM ONE UNDERARM & SERGE-FINISH THE BOTTOM EDGE

8. SERGE-SEAM THE OTHER UNDERARM

9. HEM THE BOTTOM EDGE

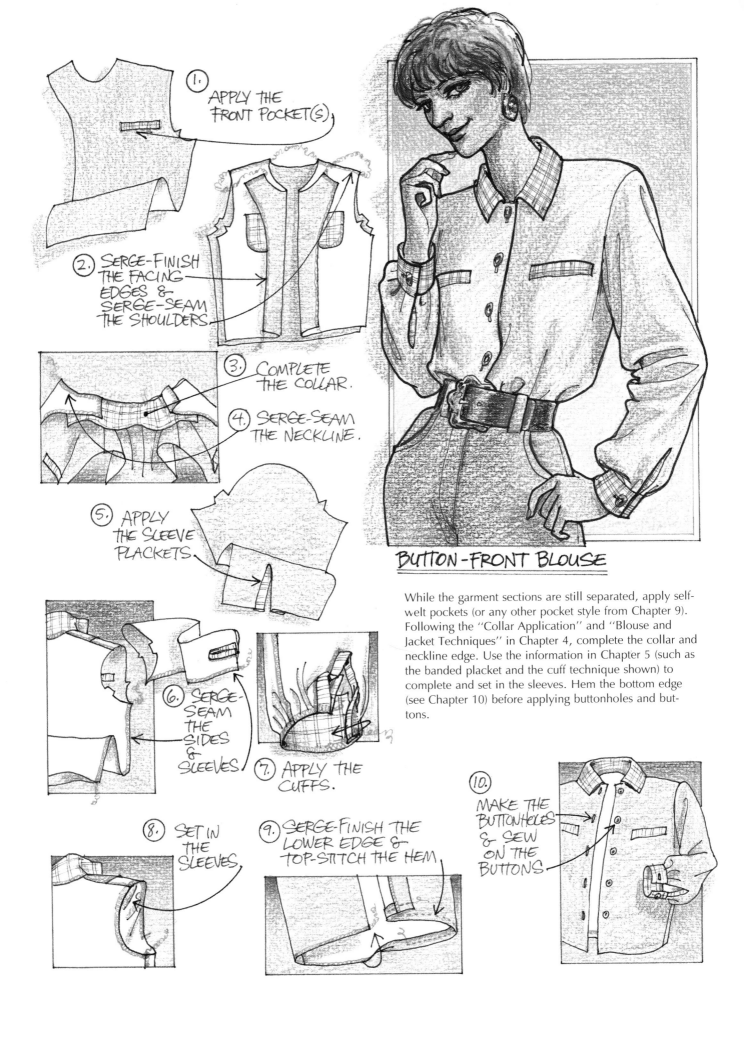

1. APPLY THE FRONT POCKET(S).

2. SERGE-FINISH THE FACING EDGES & SERGE-SEAM THE SHOULDERS.

3. COMPLETE THE COLLAR.

4. SERGE-SEAM THE NECKLINE.

5. APPLY THE SLEEVE PLACKETS.

6. SERGE-SEAM THE SIDES & SLEEVES.

7. APPLY THE CUFFS.

8. SET IN THE SLEEVES.

9. SERGE-FINISH THE LOWER EDGE & TOP-STITCH THE HEM.

10. MAKE THE BUTTONHOLES & SEW ON THE BUTTONS.

BUTTON-FRONT BLOUSE

While the garment sections are still separated, apply self-welt pockets (or any other pocket style from Chapter 9). Following the "Collar Application" and "Blouse and Jacket Techniques" in Chapter 4, complete the collar and neckline edge. Use the information in Chapter 5 (such as the banded placket and the cuff technique shown) to complete and set in the sleeves. Hem the bottom edge (see Chapter 10) before applying buttonholes and buttons.

SIMPLE PULL-ON SKIRT

Following the instructions in Chapter 7, plan for a pull-on waistband such as this wrapped and top-stitched variation. If desired, construct a slit at the center back (see Chapter 10). Apply in-seam pockets using the techniques from Chapter 9. Finish the waistband before hemming the garment (see Chapter 10 for hemming options). To hold a belt in place, add belt loops (see Chapter 11).

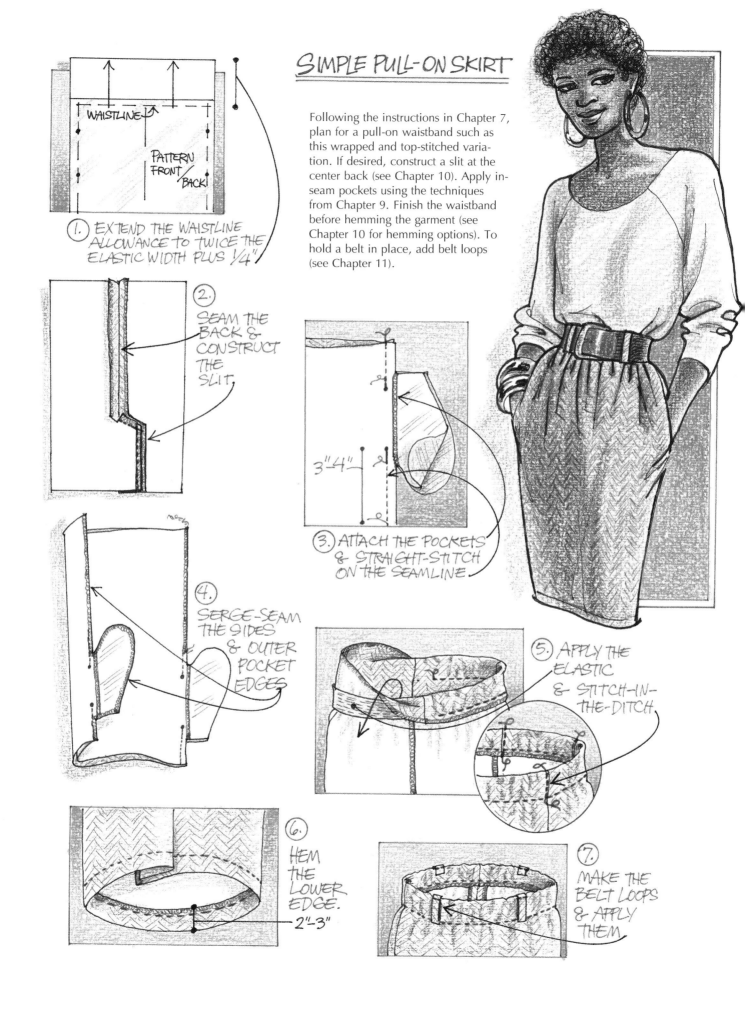

(1.) EXTEND THE WAISTLINE ALLOWANCE TO TWICE THE ELASTIC WIDTH PLUS 1/4"

WAISTLINE

PATTERN FRONT/BACK

(2.) SEAM THE BACK & CONSTRUCT THE SLIT.

(3.) ATTACH THE POCKETS & STRAIGHT-STITCH ON THE SEAMLINE.

3"-4"

(4.) SERGE-SEAM THE SIDES & OUTER POCKET EDGES

(5.) APPLY THE ELASTIC & STITCH-IN-THE-DITCH

(6.) HEM THE LOWER EDGE.

2"-3"

(7.) MAKE THE BELT LOOPS & APPLY THEM

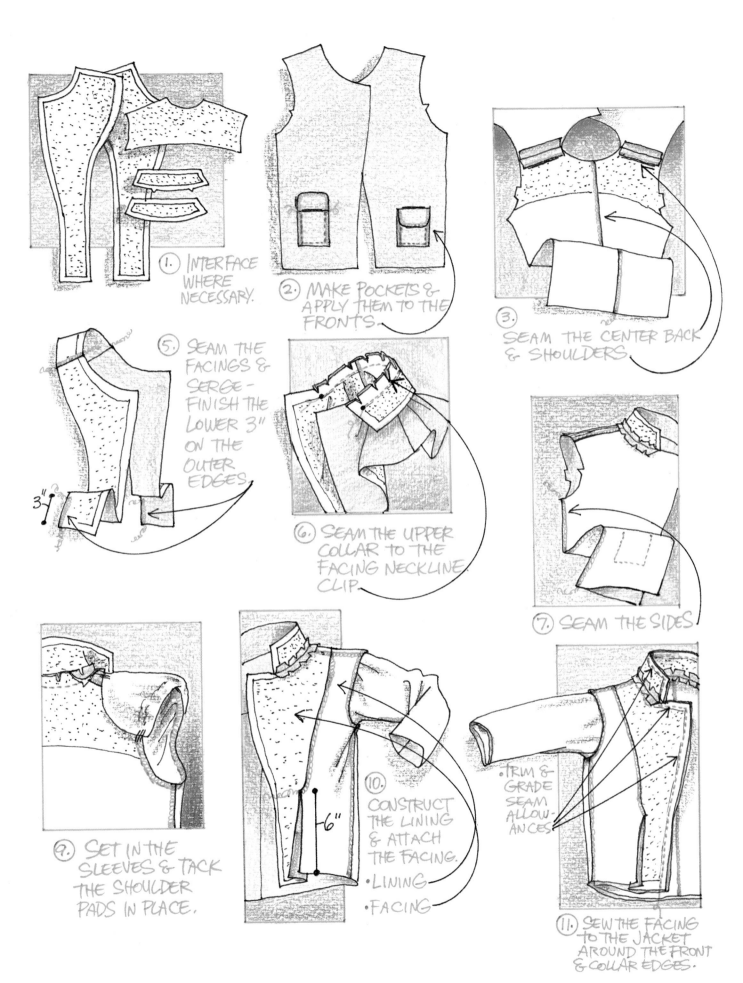

1. INTERFACE WHERE NECESSARY.

2. MAKE POCKETS & APPLY THEM TO THE FRONTS.

3. SEAM THE CENTER BACK & SHOULDERS.

5. SEAM THE FACINGS & SERGE-FINISH THE LOWER 3" ON THE OUTER EDGES.

3"

6. SEAM THE UPPER COLLAR TO THE FACING NECKLINE CLIP.

7. SEAM THE SIDES

9. SET IN THE SLEEVES & TACK THE SHOULDER PADS IN PLACE.

10. CONSTRUCT THE LINING & ATTACH THE FACING.
• LINING
• FACING

6"

• TRIM & GRADE SEAM ALLOW- ANCES

11. SEW THE FACING TO THE JACKET AROUND THE FRONT & COLLAR EDGES.

LINED, SERGE-TAILORED JACKET

Interface the garment sections as specified in your pattern (see the pointers in Chapter 2). Apply pockets (such as these double pockets) to the front pieces, following the instructions in Chapter 9. Seam the center back and shoulders (see the seam-type options in Chapter 3). Apply the undercollar to the jacket neckline and the upper collar to the completed facing in preparation for the "easy jacket lining" technique in Chapter 6. After seaming the sides, press up all the hems and seam the sleeves before setting them in. (See Chapter 5 for more sleeve information.) Then complete the easy jacket lining before hemming the garment (see Chapter 10) and applying buttonholes and buttons.

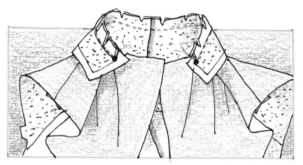

④ SEAM THE UNDERCOLLAR TO THE JACKET NECKLINE. CLIP.

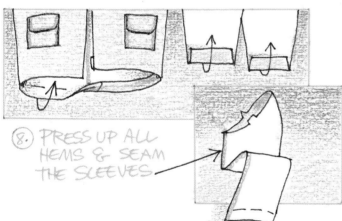

⑧ PRESS UP ALL HEMS & SEAM THE SLEEVES

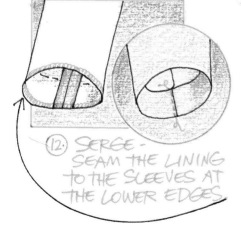

⑫ SERGE-SEAM THE LINING TO THE SLEEVES AT THE LOWER EDGES

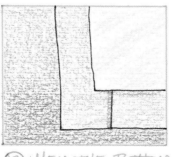

⑬ HEM THE BOTTOM EDGE.

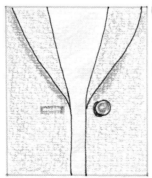

⑭ APPLY THE BUTTONHOLE(S) & BUTTON(S)

BACK-ZIPPERED DRESS WITH A WAISTLINE SEAM

Before seaming the garment, add any pockets or decorative serging to the separate piece or pieces. Select a seam type from Chapter 3, seam both shoulders, and serge-finish the center-back seam allowances. Interface and complete the facings before applying them to the neckline edge (see Chapter 4). Apply the sleeves (see Chapter 5), then seam the underarms. Seam the skirt and serge-finish the center-back seam allowances and lower edge. Complete the waistline, reinforcing the seam following the technique described in Chapter 3. Straight-stitch the center-back seam and apply the zipper (see Chapter 8). Hem the sleeves and lower edge (see Chapter 10), then, if desired, use the "folded once and buttoned" technique from Chapter 5. Finish the garment by tacking the neckline facing and adding a hook and eye and shoulder pads (see Chapter 11).

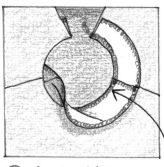

④ APPLY THE FACING TO THE NECKLINE.

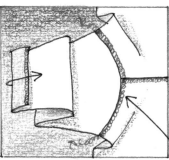

⑤ SERGE-FINISH & PRESS UP THE SLEEVE HEMS & SEAM THE SLEEVES TO THE GARMENT.

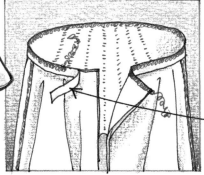

⑧ SEAM THE WAISTLINE.

SEAMS GREAT OR OTHER LIGHTWEIGHT STABILIZER.

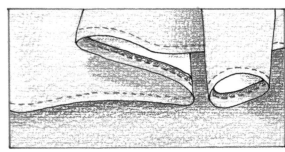

⑪ TURN UP & TOP-STITCH THE HEMS.

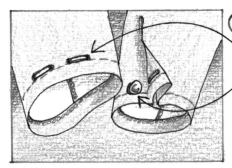

⑫ OPTIONAL: SEW BUTTONHOLES & BUTTONS TO TAPER THE SLEEVES.

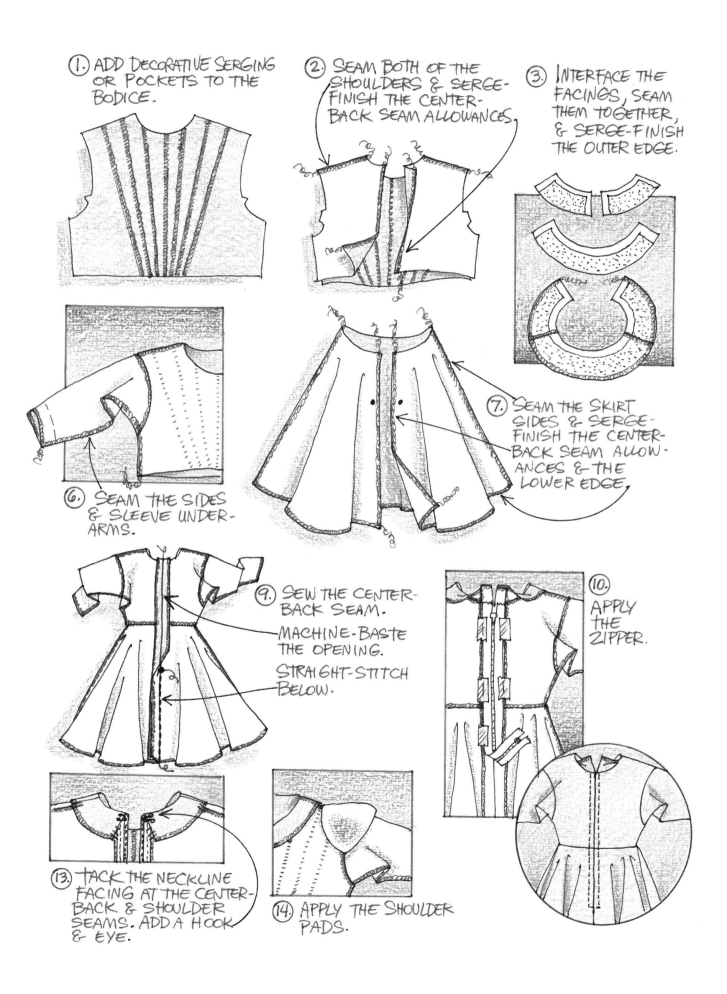

1. ADD DECORATIVE SERGING OR POCKETS TO THE BODICE.

2. SEAM BOTH OF THE SHOULDERS & SERGE-FINISH THE CENTER-BACK SEAM ALLOWANCES.

3. INTERFACE THE FACINGS, SEAM THEM TOGETHER, & SERGE-FINISH THE OUTER EDGE.

6. SEAM THE SIDES & SLEEVE UNDER-ARMS.

7. SEAM THE SKIRT SIDES & SERGE-FINISH THE CENTER-BACK SEAM ALLOW-ANCES & THE LOWER EDGE.

9. SEW THE CENTER-BACK SEAM.
MACHINE-BASTE THE OPENING.
STRAIGHT-STITCH BELOW.

10. APPLY THE ZIPPER.

13. TACK THE NECKLINE FACING AT THE CENTER-BACK & SHOULDER SEAMS. ADD A HOOK & EYE.

14. APPLY THE SHOULDER PADS.

CLASSIC TROUSERS

Begin by sewing any darts and pleats. Using the instructions in Chapter 9, sew the front-hip pockets. Serge-finish the crotch seam allowances and apply the zipper to a finished seam (see Chapter 8). Sew the outseams and serge-finish the lower edges before sewing the inseams. Straight-stitch the remainder of the crotch seam. Make belt loops (see Chapter 11) and catch the lower edges in the stitching when applying a "basic serged waistband" (see Chapter 7). Complete the trousers by folding and top-stitching the top of the loops to the waistband, sewing a hook and eye closure, and hemming (see Chapter 10 for hem options).

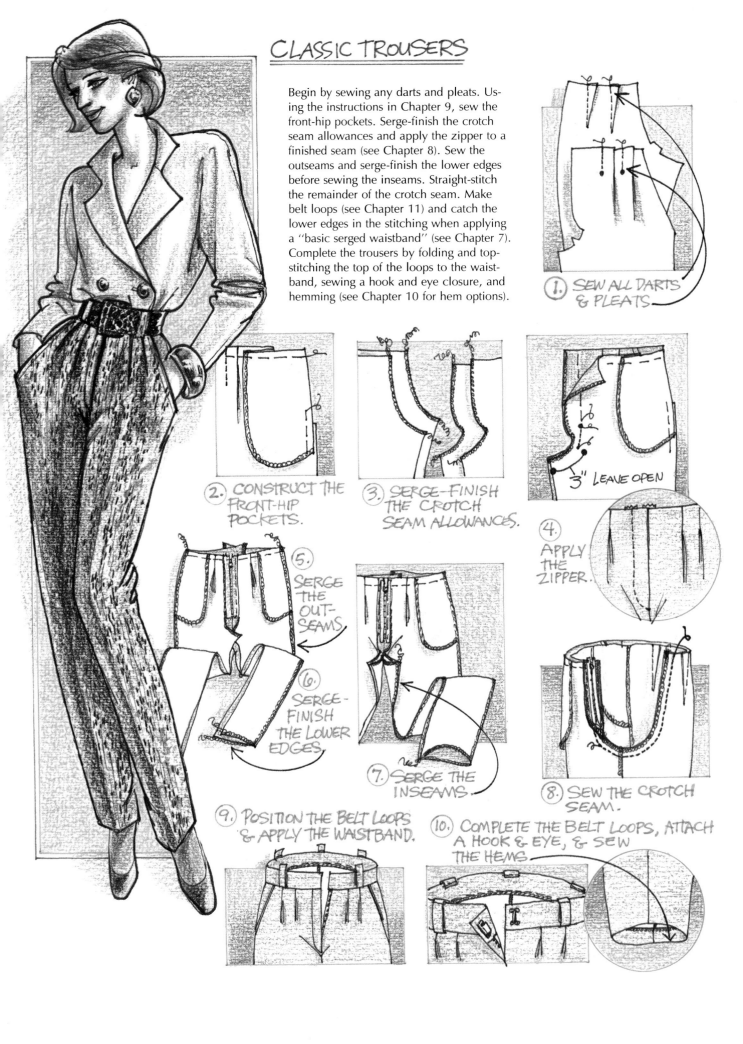

1. SEW ALL DARTS & PLEATS.

2. CONSTRUCT THE FRONT-HIP POCKETS.

3. SERGE-FINISH THE CROTCH SEAM ALLOWANCES.

4. APPLY THE ZIPPER. 3" LEAVE OPEN

5. SERGE THE OUT-SEAMS

6. SERGE-FINISH THE LOWER EDGES

7. SERGE THE INSEAMS.

8. SEW THE CROTCH SEAM.

9. POSITION THE BELT LOOPS & APPLY THE WAISTBAND.

10. COMPLETE THE BELT LOOPS, ATTACH A HOOK & EYE, & SEW THE HEMS

Plackets

When a sleeve opening is narrow or restricted by a fitted cuff, a placket is necessary so the hand can slip through easily. The speedy serged placket and keyhole openings used for necklines (see Chapter 4) can be used for sleeve plackets. In addition, several other simple placket techniques are possible. Whenever you can, apply the placket to the sleeve before completing it and attaching it to the garment.

Seamline placket

Some patterns are already designed with the placket on a seamline. Other patterns can be altered to place the placket on a seamline. In either case, serge-finish the seam allowance edges and apply the cuff flat (see the instructions on page 59) before straight-stitching the seamline to the point of the opening. (Fig. 5-11)

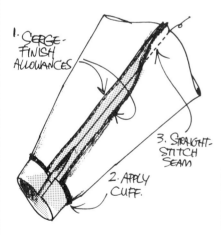

Fig. 5-11 On a seamline placket, the edges are automatically finished by the seam allowances.

Quick-serged placket

For the simplest serged placket not on a seamline, you can decoratively serge-finish the slash opening, pulling the point out in a straight line using the inside corner technique (see page 31). But if you don't want serging exposed on the outside of the garment, this technique is nearly as easy:

1. Cut a slash at the placket position and serge-finish the edge without trimming, using a narrow- to medium-width balanced stitch and pulling the corner point straight as you serge over it.

2. Fold the opening right sides together and straight-stitch a 1" dart at the point. (Fig. 5-12)

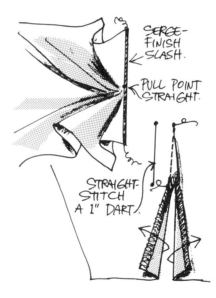

Fig. 5-12 Quickly serge a placket without exposed stitching on the outside of the garment.

3. Press the serged edges to the wrong side.

Banded placket

You can simultaneously finish the slash opening and add durability by serging a band to the edge as follows:

1. Using the lengthwise grain of the fabric, cut a strip 1" wide by the length of the opening.

2. Fold the band wrong sides together and serge-seam it to the opening with the sleeve on top. At the point of the opening, hold the fabric straight out in front, using the inside corner technique, while serging over it. (Fig. 5-13)

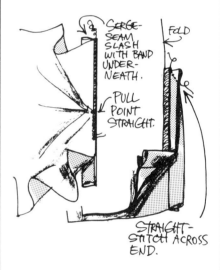

Fig. 5-13 Use a narrow band to neatly finish the placket edge.

> **On lightweight fabrics, use a decorative rolled edge to serge-seam the band. When the sleeve is rolled up, you'll see that it is neatly finished on the inside, too.**

3. Fold the band right sides together and straight-stitch diagonally across the end to reinforce the point.

Bound placket

The bound sleeve placket is similar to the keyhole opening done with a narrow binding, except the binding strip is cut wider and the second long edge is turned under for a clean finish on both the right and wrong sides of the sleeve.

1. Cut a binding strip 1" wide by the length of the opening. Use a bias woven or a crossgrain knit fabric. Serge-finish one long edge of the strip and press it to the wrong side.

> For a decorative effect, use a contrasting color binding fabric. Select a plaid or stripe to complement a solid color.

2. With right sides together and the sleeve on top, serge-seam the strip to the opening using a medium-width stitch. Pull the corner point out straight in front as you serge over it. (Fig. 5-14)

3. Wrap the binding strip around the seam allowance to the wrong side. Stitch-in-the-ditch from the right side to secure. Press the point to ease in the fabric at the curve.

4. If the corner point does not ease smoothly into a curve, fold the binding right sides together and straight-stitch vertically through the end of the binding for a flat finish. (Fig. 5-15)

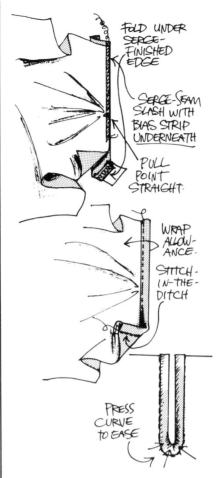

Fig. 5-14 Bind the placket with a bias strip.

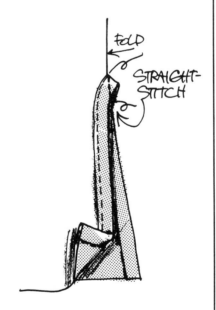

Fig. 5-15 Straight-stitch through the binding vertically if it cannot be eased around the point.

Mock-tailored placket

Because a tailored shirt placket requires the precision of straight-stitching, it is very difficult to complete one accurately using the serger. Instead, try this simple technique to simulate the look:

1. Cut a band on the lengthwise fabric grain 2" wide by the length of the opening.

2. Serge the band to the placket opening, following step 2 (page 57) for the banded placket.

3. Fold the band to the wrong side and press it into position. With the placket spread flat, straight-stitch two parallel rows along the placket edge closest to the center of the sleeve, 1/8" from the fold and again 1/2" away. Stop even with the point at the end of the opening. (Fig. 5-16) Pull the thread ends to the underside, knot them, and trim the excess.

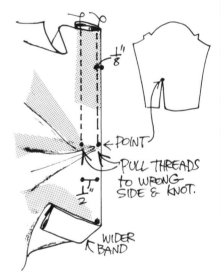

Fig. 5-16 For a mock tailored placket, straight-stitch to the point.

4. Fold the placket back into position. At the top, top-stitch through all layers to secure the folded end of the band and form a point. (Fig. 5-17)

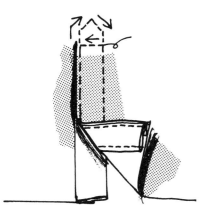

Fig. 5-17 Top-stitch a pointed end, catching the top fold of the band as you stitch across it.

Cuffs

Depending on the style of the garment, sleeve cuffs can be fitted around the wrist, as on a tailored shirt, or loose, as on many coats. When the cuff is fitted (unless it is ribbing), a placket opening is necessary. Loose cuffs usually do not have openings and are finished in a circle as a band or hem.

Quickest cuff

A cuff can be serge-seamed to a garment quickly and easily:
1. Interface and serge-seam the cuffs, turn them right side out, and press.

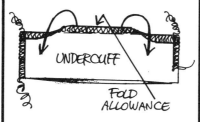

Fig. 5-18 Wrap the outside corners toward the cuff before serge-seaming the sides.

2. Apply a seamline or quick-serged sleeve placket, following the instructions on pages 57 to 58. Prepare the lower sleeve edge, following the pattern instructions, gathering or pleating if required.

3. Place the right side of the cuff against the right side of the sleeve, wrapping the sleeve seam allowances around the ends of the cuff. (Fig. 5-19)

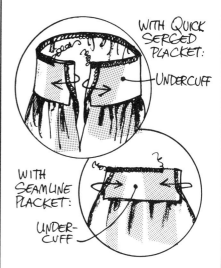

Fig. 5-19 Wrap the seam allowances toward the undercuff before serge-seaming the cuff to the sleeve.

4. Serge-seam through all layers. Turn the cuff right side out.

Clean-finished cuff

For other placket types or when you don't want the serged seaming exposed on the inside of the garment (if you will be rolling up the sleeves, for example), use this method to position all the edges neatly inside the cuff:

1. Serge-seam the outer edge of the cuff if it is cut in two pieces. Press under the raw edge of the undercuff along the remaining long seamline.

2. With the cuff right sides together, serge-seam both ends, wrapping the outer edge allowance if there is one. (Fig. 5-20)

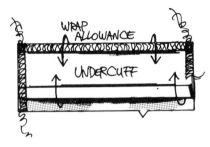

Fig. 5-20 Serge-seam the sides of the cuff with the undercuff seam allowance folded to the wrong side.

3. Prepare the lower sleeve edge, including any gathers or tucks.

4. Turn the cuff right side out and pin it, right sides together, with the outer cuff against the right side of the sleeve, matching the notches and opening edges. Hold the undercuff away from the stitching line. (Fig. 5-21)

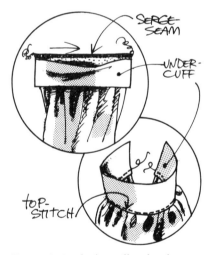

Fig. 5-21 Apply the cuff to the sleeve right sides together. Then press the seam allowance to the inside of the cuff and top-stitch.

5. Serge-seam, press the allowances to the inside of the cuff, and top-stitch near the cuff edge to catch the fold on the underside.

Ribbed cuff

A band of ribbing can be applied as a sleeve cuff on either a knit or a woven garment.

> **To measure for a ribbed cuff, place the ribbing comfortably around the wrist or cut it equal to the wrist measurement, plus 1/2" for seam allowances. The finished cuff width should be 2" to 3-1/2" wide plus seam allowances.**

Although a ribbed cuff can be attached to the sleeve using a circular application (see page 43 for neckline finishes), you will usually apply it using the flat construction method:

1. Purchase or knit a ribbed cuff that is finished on one long edge or use a doubled band of ribbing. Using a long, wide, balanced stitch with the ribbing on top, serge-seam the ribbing right sides together to the lower sleeve edge.

> **For a blouson effect on a ribbed sleeve, add 1/2" to 1" to the lower edge when cutting out the garment. (Fig. 5-22)**

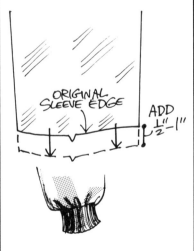

Fig. 5-22 Cut out longer sleeves to create a blouson effect.

2. Finger-press the seam allowance toward the garment.

> **To prevent stretching when fabric is eased to the ribbing, do NOT top-stitch next to the ribbing through the seam allowance on the underside.**

3. After applying the sleeves, serge-seam one underarm seam, finish the bottom edge of the garment, and serge-seam the other underarm. When completing the underarm seam at the cuff edge, stretch horizontally across the seamline in front of the foot to align the layers and produce the neatest finish. (Fig. 5-23)

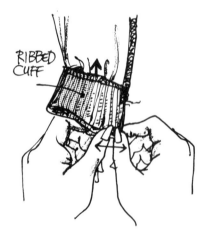

Fig. 5-23 Hold your thumbs side by side at the lower corner, pulling gently in opposite directions to align the layers.

To neatly finish the underarm seam without having to secure the thread ends after serge-seaming, fold the cuff right sides together and serge onto it for two stitches. Raise the presser foot and bring the thread chain underneath the foot, straight out in front. Serge slowly over the chain for about 1" before trimming off the remainder. (Fig. 5-24)

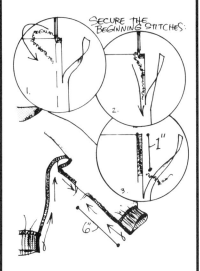

Fig. 5-24 For a neatly finished underarm seam, begin at both ends, securing the beginning stitches and overlapping on the sleeve.

Continue serge-seaming for about 6". Repeat the same procedure from the lower edge of the garment and serge-seam the remainder of the underarm, overlapping the stitching for about 1" to secure.

Banded cuff

When a band is applied to the garment neckline (see page 47), the sleeves are often finished to match. Banded cuffs are usually applied flat, following the same technique as the neckline application, before the underarm seam is stitched. (Fig. 5-25)

Fig. 5-25 Apply banded cuffs to the sleeves to match the neckline finish.

Folded cuff

Most often used on straight-cut coat sleeves or short sleeves (as well as for pants), the folded cuff is created by simply extending the hem twice the depth of the desired cuff width plus the hem allowance. This cuff style is always applied after the sleeve has been seamed into a circle.

1. Cut the sleeves using a pattern with a folded cuff or adding twice the cuff depth to the bottom edge. (Fig. 5-26)

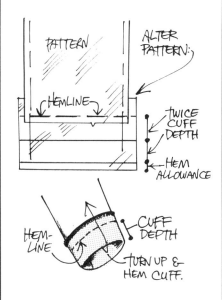

Fig. 5-26 Make a folded cuff by adding to the lower sleeve edge.

2. Serge-finish the raw edge and fold the sleeve so one cuff width extends below the hemline.

3. Hem the sleeve using straight-stitching or blindhemming.

4. Turn up and press the cuff on the hemline. To hold the cuff in position, stitch-in-the-ditch on the cuff seamlines or hand-tack on the seamlines between the cuff and the garment, 1/2" below the cuff edge. (Fig. 5-27)

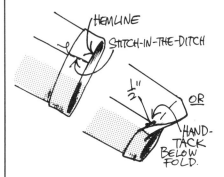

Fig. 5-27 Secure the cuff after folding.

Other Sleeve Finishes

Chapter 10 outlines serged hems and edges, and any of the techniques included there can be used to finish sleeves. Several other finishing techniques can also be used.

Facing

When the pattern calls for a facing, use the techniques for a round neckline facing (page 39).

Because a facing can be cut from a different fabric than the garment, it is often used on sleeves for a decorative effect. To display a contrasting facing on the outside of a garment, serge-seam with the right side of the facing against the wrong side of the sleeve edge or use a wide contrasting facing on the underside for contrasting roll-up sleeves. (Fig. 5-28)

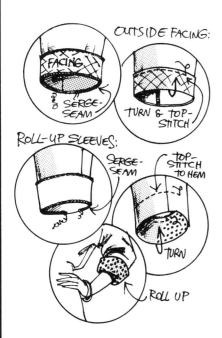

Fig. 5-28 Feature a contrasting facing on the right or wrong side of the garment.

For a lined roll-up sleeve with a faced effect, cut out each sleeve twice, in contrasting colors, and serge-seam the lower ends right sides together. Then serge the underarm seams and apply the sleeves using the circular method. (See Fig. 5-29)

Fig. 5-29 Use a doubled sleeve for a contrasting roll-up.

Binding

Bind sleeve edges to match a bound neckline. Follow the guidelines and techniques that begin on page 45.

Easy elastic casing

Quickly make a neat elastic casing to gather the edges of either long or short sleeves:

1. Fit 3/8"-wide elastic around your wrist or arm and mark the length needed—do not cut it.

2. Allow for a 5/8"-wide hem and serge-finish the hem edge.

If your pattern was not designed with a gathered sleeve opening, add blousing ease (see Fig. 5-22) as well as the 5/8"-wide hem allowance to the lower edge when cutting out.

3. Press the hem to the wrong side and insert the elastic. Straight-stitch to secure one end. (Fig. 5-30)

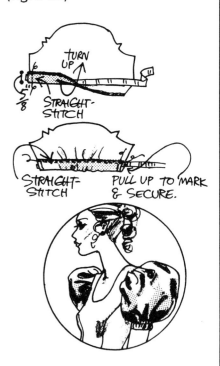

Fig. 5-30 Serge-finish the hem edge to make a quick elastic casing.

4. Straight-stitch 1/8" from the upper hem edge, forming a casing. Do not catch the elastic in the stitching.

5. Pull the elastic to the mark made in step 1 and secure the end with straight-stitching.

6. Cut the elastic and seam the underarm, catching the ends of the elastic in the stitching.

To add a lace trim or a contrasting ruffle to the bottom of the elastic casing, complete the previous steps 1 and 2. Fold up the hem, lap the serge-finished edge of the lace or ruffle under it, and top-stitch close to the folded edge. (Fig. 5-31) Insert the elastic, straight-stitch one end, and follow the remaining steps as outlined to complete the sleeve.

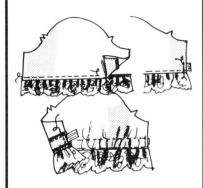

Fig. 5-31 To add a ruffle, straight-stitch it to the fold before adding the elastic and finishing the casing.

Flounced elastic casing

Position the casing away from the sleeve edge if you want a gathered flounce below the casing. Before cutting, extend the sleeve from the hemline an amount equal to twice the desired flounce depth plus 5/8" for the casing. (Fig. 5-32)

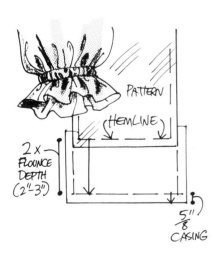

Fig. 5-32 Alter the pattern to add a flounce below the elastic casing.

Because the inside of the flounce will be visible at times when being worn, follow the steps outlined below to serge-seam the underarm and complete the casing in a circle to hide the seam allowance.

1. Fit 3/8"-wide elastic around your wrist or arm and measure the length needed, allowing at least a 1/2" overlap.

2. Serge-finish the lower sleeve edge and fold up the flounce depth plus 5/8".

3. Straight-stitch 1/8" from the serge-finished edge, leaving an opening for threading the elastic. (Fig. 5-33)

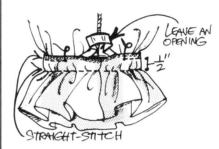

Fig. 5-33 Fold up the casing and flounce and straight-stitch before inserting the elastic.

4. Straight-stitch 1/2" from the first row of stitching, overlapping the ends and forming the casing.

5. Thread the elastic through the casing, overlapping and seaming the ends together. Straight-stitch the opening closed.

Tucked

Serge dainty tucks on a sleeve hem to narrow the opening and add an interesting cuff detail. Face the sleeve for the least bulky application, following the steps outlined below (Fig. 5-34):

Fig. 5-34 Tuck the bottom of a sleeve and face the opening.

1. Using a disappearing marker (test first), draw tuck lines on the wrong side of the sleeve, extending from the raw edge to 2" past the seam allowance on the lower edge.

Plan the number of tucks you will be making and space them an equal distance apart on the sleeve edge. Remember that each tuck will narrow the sleeve opening by twice the distance of the stitch width, so be sure the completed sleeve will still slip comfortably over your hand.

2. Fold the sleeve right sides together on each tuck mark. Beginning at the raw edge, serge the tucks using a wide, balanced stitch. At the end of each tuck, lift the needle and the presser foot, pull the fabric behind the needle, and chain off. Secure the thread chains on the end toward the sleeve. (Fig. 5-35)

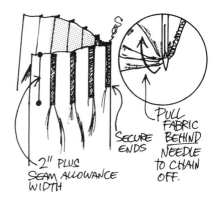

Fig. 5-35 Serge tucks an equal distance apart at the sleeve edge.

3. Using the tucked sleeve as a pattern, cut a facing 2" wide plus the seam allowance. Serge-finish the raw edge and, after sewing the sleeve underarm seam, apply the facing using the circular method.

> **To apply decorative tucks on the outside of the sleeve, follow the steps given previously except serge along the folds with a flatlock stitch and wrong sides together. (Don't let the stitches hang off the edge, but don't cut the fabric with the knives, either.) The needle thread will create a ladder effect on the wrong side and a tuck will form under the stitches. (Fig. 5-36)**

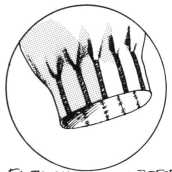

Fig. 5-36 Loosen the needle tension and tighten the lower looper tension to serge decorative tucks.

Folded once and buttoned

If the bottom of the sleeve is too full or if you want to add a fashionable detail, fold a tuck in the sleeve, make two buttonholes, and sew on a button:

1. Seam the underarm and hem the sleeve.

2. Make a pleat at the outer sleeve edge, taking out the desired amount of fullness—usually about 1-1/2" wide. (Fig. 5-37)

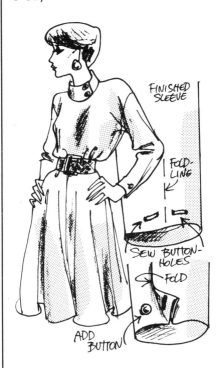

Fig. 5-37 Narrow a sleeve opening by folding and buttoning.

3. Sew a separate buttonhole through both layers of the pleat and attach a button to the underlap.

Mock ruffle edging

On loosely woven fabric such as gauze, you can quickly ruffle the edge and serge-seam a fold to replicate an applied ruffle:

1. Lettuce the sleeve edge in a circle using a satin-length rolled edge and stretching firmly while serging.

2. Fold the edge at least 1-1/4" to the right side and serge-seam the fold using a wide, balanced stitch. (Fig. 5-38)

Fig. 5-38 Add a mock ruffle to gauze or other loosely woven sleeve edges.

3. Gently press the seam allowances toward the sleeve and topstitch from the right side, if desired. Steam the ruffles.

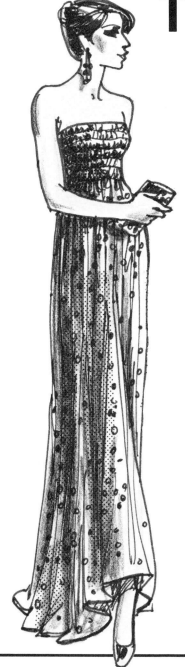

CHAPTER 6

HANDY SERGER CONSTRUCTION TECHNIQUES

CHAPTER 6

Handy Serger Construction Techniques

Gathering ✂ Shirring ✂ Ruffles ✂ Tucks ✂ Pleats ✂ Simple Lining Techniques

Keep in mind that with most serge-gathering techniques, the finished seam allowance will be the width of the serged stitch. This may limit its use for loosely woven or extremely ravelly fabrics or where wider seam allowances are desired. **(Fig. 6-1)**

Fig. 6-1 Serge-gather whenever wider seam allowances are not important.

Gathering

Use your serger to speed up the sometimes tedious gathering process and it will finish the edge of the fabric for you at the same time.

For gathering, adjust your serger for the widest balanced stitch. Before serge-gathering the actual garment piece, test the amount of gathering on fabric scraps. The weight and thickness of the fabric and the length to be gathered will determine which technique to use. In general:

✂ Lightweight fabric will gather more easily than heavier fabric which often won't gather but can be eased.

✂ Soft fabric will gather more easily than stiffer fabric.

✂ A single layer will gather more easily than two layers.

Differential-feed gathering

Use the differential feed to gather lighter-weight fabrics or ease heavier fabrics. For maximum gathering:

✂ Select the highest (2.0) setting.

✂ Use the longest stitch.

✂ Tighten the needle tension (both tensions with two needles).

To gather or ease one fabric layer to another, place the fabric to be gathered underneath and serge-seam, holding the upper layer taut. (See Fig. 3-28) Some machine models have an optional gathering accessory which does this automatically.

Tension gathering

Even without differential-feed you can serge-gather lighter-weight fabric by adjusting to the longest stitch and tightening the needle tension(s) almost completely. For less gathering, shorten the stitch length. (Fig. 6-2)

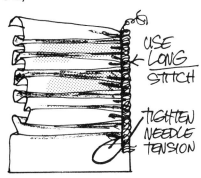

Fig. 6-2 Use tension gathering on lightweight fabric.

Gather or ease one layer of fabric to another using the method described previously for differential-feed gathering.

For quick tension gathering without changing the tension settings, with your finger press the needle thread against the serger either above or below the needle tension control. (Test on your model to find the spot that works best.) Be careful not to apply so much pressure that the

thread breaks. Readjust to the original tension simply by removing the pressure from the thread. (Fig. 6-3)

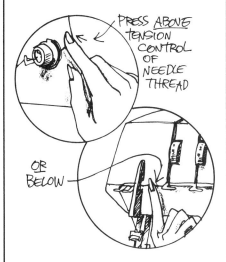

Fig. 6-3 Test the best location on your machine to apply quick tension gathering.

For maximum gathering, allow the fabric to feed freely into the machine. For additional gathering with both the differential-feed and tension methods, ease-plus by holding the fabric behind the presser foot as you serge. (See Fig. 3-6)

Needle-thread gathering

Easily gather short sections of fabric by pulling the needle thread of the serged stitching.

Use buttonhole twist thread in a size 14/90 needle for a stronger, more durable gathering thread.

When you need just a little more easing to fit one piece to another, use a pin to pick up a stitch anywhere along the needle-line (or both needlelines of a 3/4-thread stitch) and pull to gather the edge slightly. (See Fig. 5-4)

Use this technique to gather any short section:

1. Loosen the needle tension slightly before serge-finishing the edge.

2. Secure the serged thread chain on one end.

3. Pull out the chain on the opposite end to find the shortest thread (the needle thread) in the chain. Pull it to gather the edge. (On a 3/4-thread stitch, pull both needle threads.) (Fig. 6-4)

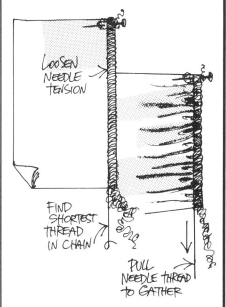

Fig. 6-4 Gather short sections by pulling the needle thread.

This technique also works well for removing serged stitching. Cut the chain off one end. At the other end, simply pull the needle thread(s) completely out of the serged stitching and the looper threads will fall away.

Combination gathering

To maintain a wider seam allowance, use serge-gathering in combination with straight-stitching:

1. Without trimming, serge-finish the edge to be gathered. Use a long, medium- to narrow-width, balanced 3-thread stitch and loosen the needle thread tension slightly.

2. Machine-baste on or just inside the seamline.

3. Matching any markings, pin the serge-finished piece against the corresponding garment area. Gather it by simultaneously pulling the machine-basting bobbin thread and the serger needle thread. Distribute the gathers evenly. (Fig. 6-5)

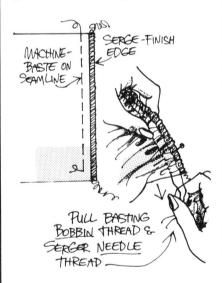

Fig. 6-5 Use combination gathering to maintain a wider seam allowance.

4. Straight-stitch the seam. Serge-finish the seam allowances together.

> **When using combination gathering to insert sleeves, trim the seam allowances to 1/4" between the underarm notches as you serge-finish the edges together.**

Elastic gathering

Quickly gather an edge by serging over stretched clear elastic. Place the elastic on top of the fabric and serge through both layers. Use the longest stitch and stretch the elastic as you serge (it can stretch up to three times its original length). The more the elastic is stretched, the more the fabric will gather.

1. Mark both the elastic and the fabric to be gathered in even sections. On the elastic, allow 1" to 2" before the first mark to begin smoothly and anchor the stitches.

2. Serge a few stitches on the elastic, then insert the fabric under it at the first mark.

3. Serge, stretching the elastic to match the remaining marks. (Fig. 6-6)

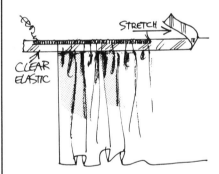

Fig. 6-6 Gather an edge using clear elastic. Stretch more for more gathering.

> **When a precise amount of gathering is not required (on a ruffle, for example), eliminate testing and premeasuring by serge-gathering a long strip of fabric and cutting the gathered piece to the desired length.**

Filler-cord gathering

For better control when gathering medium- to heavy-weight fabric, serge over a filler cord, such as crochet thread, buttonhole twist, or pearl cotton. Use a medium-length, balanced 3-thread stitch.

1. Place the filler under the back and over the front of the presser foot between the needle and the knives (or thread the filler through a specialty foot if one is available for your model). (See Fig. 4-3) Serge over the filler for a few stitches before inserting the fabric under the foot.

2. Serge over the filler, guiding it between the needle and knives, being careful not to cut it or stitch through it.

3. At the end, raise the needle and the presser foot, pull the filler behind the needle, and chain off without stitching through it. (Fig. 6-7)

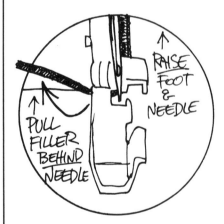

Fig. 6-7 Chain off without stitching through the filler.

4. Secure one end of the filler by wrapping it around a pin, knotting it, or stitching through it for several stitches when you begin to serge. Pull the opposite end to gather.

Try these filler-cord gathering variations:

✂ For quick gathering, use the thread chain as filler cord. Before using the method previously described, serge a thread chain approximately the same length as the area to be gathered. Raise the presser foot and guide the chain under the back and over the front of the foot. Place the fabric under the foot and serge over the chain, holding it taut to prevent stitching through it or cutting it. After completing the serging, pull the chain to gather. (Fig. 6-8)

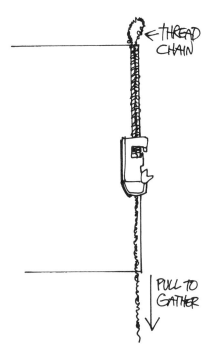

Fig. 6-8 Use a thread chain as a handy filler cord.

✂ Let the machine help with the gathering as you serge. Use the previous thread-chain gathering method or stitch through the cord as you begin. Then hold the filler taut and the fabric will gather automatically as you serge. (Fig. 6-9)

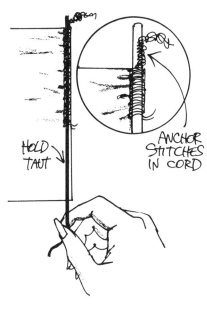

Fig. 6-9 Let the serger gather as you stitch over taut filler.

✂ For more controlled gathering, serge using a 3/4-thread stitch with two needles. Guide the filler between the needles without stitching into it. The stitches will hold the filler in position along the needleline, so the gathering is more even. (Fig. 6-10)

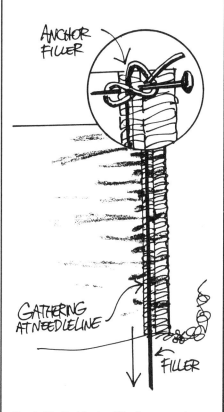

Fig. 6-10 Guide the filler between the needles of a 3/4-thread stitch for more gathering control.

Shirring

Use your serger to make stretchable parallel rows of gathering (called shirring) on cuffs, waistlines, necklines, or anywhere away from the fabric edge.

Chainstitched shirring

If your serger model has a 2-thread double chainstitch, use it to shirr lightweight fabric by serging with elastic thread in the looper. For additional shirring, set the differential feed on 2.0 (or ease-plus) and tighten the looper thread slightly. Use one of these two chainstitched shirring methods:

✄ Top-stitch the shirring rows from the right side. This is possible only when the machine's upper looper and knife can be disengaged. Check your owner's manual. (Fig. 6-11)

✄ Fold the fabric right sides together and chainstitch rows close to the fold. With this method, the fabric will be narrowed by the amount that is taken up in the resulting tuck.

Elastic shirring

If the fabric is medium- to heavy-weight or if your serger model does not have a double chainstitch, use the previous method for filler-cord gathering to create shirring. Serge-gather over 1/8" elastic, elastic cording, or elastic thread (two or more strands if it's lightweight).

1. Cut out the garment and mark parallel shirring lines on the wrong side of the fabric by using a disappearing marker or by press-marking. Space the lines about 3/4" apart so the presser foot will fit easily between the rows.

2. Adjust your serger for a 2- or 3-thread flatlock. Use a stitch wide enough to serge over the elastic without cutting or stitching through it so the elastic can be pulled up easily. Disengage the knife, if possible, to avoid cutting the elastic or the fabric.

3. Place the elastic under the back and over the front of the presser foot. Serge over the elastic for a few stitches.

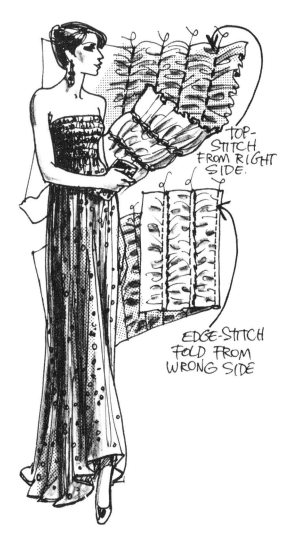

TOP-STITCH FROM RIGHT SIDE.

EDGE-STITCH FOLD FROM WRONG SIDE

Fig. 6-11 With elastic thread in the looper, the double chainstitch will create shirring.

4. Fold the fabric right sides together along one marked line and place it under the elastic and the presser foot. Serge over the elastic and the folded edge, using the filler-cord gathering techniques on page 68. Allow the flatlocking stitches to hang off the fabric edge when serging. (Fig. 6-12)

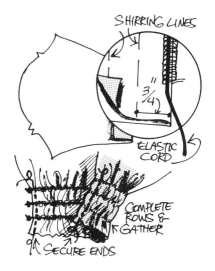

Fig. 6-12 Flatlock over elastic and the folded shirring lines. After gathering, secure the ends by straight-stitching in the seam allowances. Adjust the fullness.

Leave a tail of about 3" on each end of the elastic for easy manipulation when gathering.

5. Complete all rows, repeating steps 3 and 4.

6. Straight-stitch in the seam allowance on one side to secure the elastic. Then pull up on the elastic the desired amount. Pull out the fabric to distribute the fullness evenly and straight-stitch in the second seam allowance to secure.

You can also serge-shirr using a medium-length, balanced 3-thread stitch over the folds instead of a flatlock as in the previous step 4. In this case, the serging will take up additional fabric—about twice the width of the serged stitch, so shirr the fabric before cutting out the garment. Use a disappearing marker to outline the pattern piece on the fabric. Shirr the width of the pattern piece, then outline the pattern piece again to correct for the amount taken up by the serging. (Fig. 6-13) Cut out the garment, being careful not to cut the elastic tails. Then pull up the shirring as in the previous step 6.

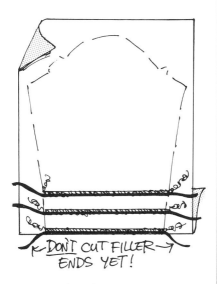

Fig. 6-13 When shirring with a balanced stitch, sew only the length needed. Then cut out the piece flat before gathering.

For foolproof gathering, begin with a long strip of elastic. Mark the finished shirring length on the elastic, allowing about 3" at the beginning. After serge-shirring and securing one elastic end, pull the other end to gather until the mark is exposed. Secure and cut the remaining end. (Fig. 6-14)

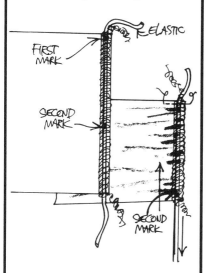

Fig. 6-14 Mark the elastic for the length desired. Gather to the mark after stitching.

Ruffles

Use ruffles to add fun and flair to many types of garments. Serge-finish one side of a single ruffle or both sides of a double ruffle using any of the edge-finishing methods (or one of the hemming techniques) featured in Chapter 10. Gather the opposite long edge of a single ruffle using one of the previously described serge-gathering techniques. Gather the center of a double ruffle following the techniques outlined for serge-shirring over the fold, but serge only one row and use any filler-cord recommended for serge-gathering. (Fig. 6-15)

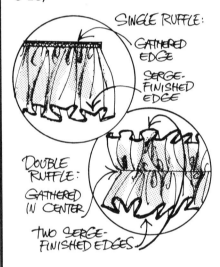

Fig. 6-15 Seam a single ruffle to the garment. Top-stitch a double ruffle.

When making ruffles:

✄ Finish the edge or edges of the ruffle strip before gathering.

✄ Make a long ruffle by seaming the ends of several sections together before finishing the edge or edges. Serge-seam using a narrow balanced stitch or a rolled edge.

> **Save time by using the same stitch for seaming as you'll use for finishing the ruffle edge.**

✄ Cut ruffles on the bias for the prettiest effect—they'll ruffle more fully and wrinkle less. Before cutting, test the finishing technique. Using some techniques (a rolled edge, for example) on certain bias-cut fabric may be difficult. If so, use another finishing technique or cut the ruffle on the crosswise grain.

> **If a rolled edge pulls away from the edge of a bias ruffle, widen the stitch, lengthen it, or do both. The wider stitch will also roll the edge completely to the underside, preventing the threads from poking out through the stitching at the edge.**

✄ Apply a single ruffle by serge-seaming it to the fabric edge or inserting it in a seam. Press the seam allowance toward the garment, and top-stitch, if desired. (Fig. 6-16)

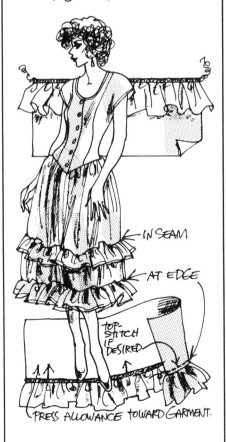

Fig. 6-16 Serge-seam to apply a single ruffle.

✄ When using a wide single ruffle as a neckline finish, use the technique on page 46 or try this quicker circular method:

1. Place the right side of the ruffle against the wrong side of the neckline edge. Serge-seam using a wide, balanced stitch.

2. Fold the ruffle to the right side, pressing the seam allowance toward the garment. Understitch. (Fig. 6-17)

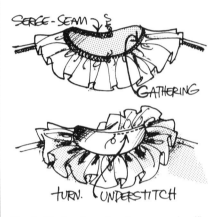

Fig. 6-17 Apply a circular-seamed ruffle at the neckline to hide the seam allowance.

✄ Apply a double ruffle by top-stitching over the center gathering stitches.

When you apply a double ruffle to a neckline edge, it will hide any serge-finishing or hemming underneath. If you're facing the neckline, simply place the facing and garment wrong sides together and serge-finish. Without a facing, serge-finish the edge, turn it to the right side, and top-stitch for a clean finish on the underside. (Fig. 6-18)

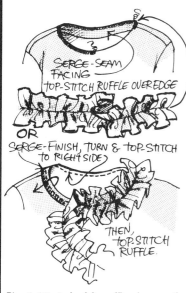

Fig. 6-18 A double ruffle also neatly finishes a neckline edge.

✄ For a lightweight, stretchable double ruffle, use narrow clear elastic as the gathering filler cord. When top-stitching the ruffle to the garment, use a narrow zigzag or twin-needle stitch for stretch-ability.

✄ Try a double ruffle with the gathering closer to one edge, forming a header after it is top-stitched in place. (Fig. 6-19)

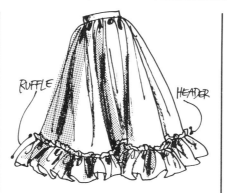

Fig. 6-19 Gather a double ruffle closer to one edge to create a single ruffle with a header.

Tucks

Add design detail anywhere on a garment using serged tucks. Some tips:

✄ Mark and serge the tucks before the garment piece is cut out.

✄ Mark parallel lines on the right side of the fabric with a disappearing marker, or use the presser foot as a guide. (Fig. 6-20)

✄ Serged tucks are the same width as the serged stitch so they can vary from dainty rolled-edge pintucks to tucks as wide as your serger's widest stitch.

✄ The tucks can be hidden on the inside of the garment or exposed decoratively on the outside. (See the tucked sleeve finish on page 63).

When using decorative thread on a garment, place it in both loopers if the stitching will be visible from both sides. Use it in the upper looper only (with matching thread in the needle and lower looper) if the under-side won't be visible or when using a rolled-edge stitch.

Fig. 6-20 Serge tucks anywhere on the garment before it is cut out.

Try these decorative tuck options:

✄ Serge crisscrossed pintucks using intersecting parallel lines to form a lattice pattern. (Fig. 6-21)

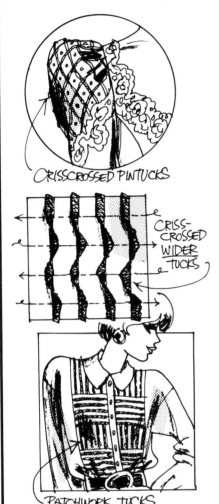

CRISSCROSSED PINTUCKS

CRISS-CROSSED WIDER TUCKS

PATCHWORK TUCKS

Fig. 6-21 Create decorative interest with tuck variations.

✄ Crisscross rows of wider tucks by straight-stitching over the tucks in alternate directions.

✄ Cut sections of tucked fabric and seam them into a patchwork design.

Serge-finish the edges of straight-stitched tucks for a decorative effect. (Fig. 6-22) A rolled edge finish over the fold will keep the tuck creased. For scalloped tucks, use the sewing machine's blindhem stitch over a rolled edge (see page 112).

ROLLED EDGE

Fig. 6-22 Use a crisp serged edging for straight-stitched tucks.

Pleats

Use a rolled edge to hold the creases on pleated skirts and pant fronts. This technique works especially well for knits and natural-fiber fabrics that will not hold a permanent crease. Follow these guidelines:

✄ Finish the garment hem before serge-creasing the pleats; then construct the remainder of the garment after creasing.

✄ Use thread to match the fabric and adjust for a medium-length rolled edge.

✄ Use the narrowest possible stitch width.

✄ Press the pleat or crease and serge-finish the folded edge, being careful not to cut the fabric. (Fig. 6-23)

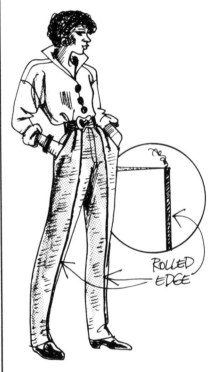

ROLLED EDGE

Fig. 6-23 Serge over the fold to hold a pleat or crease.

✂ Serge from the same direction to ensure stitch and color uniformity.

> **To hold all of the creases in a pleated skirt, serge-finish the folds on both the right and wrong sides of the garment. (Fig. 6-24)**

Fig. 6-24 On a pleated skirt, serge-finish all the folds.

Simple Lining Techniques

With a serger, you no longer need to avoid lining most garments because of the extra steps and time-consuming techniques traditionally required. The serger enables you to eliminate much of the hand-stitching and speed up the construction time.

> **When lining a garment constructed of loosely woven or ravelly fabric, serge-finish the seam allowances of the garment even though they will be enclosed. This prevents raveling during construction and fitting and adds durability during the life of the garment.**

When lining a garment, use the widest medium-length balanced 3- or 4-thread stitch for both seaming and finishing. Most lining seams and edges can be serged, with the exception of a zipper opening. For that seam, serge-finish the allowances, straight-stitch to the end of the zipper opening, and press the seam open.

Quick dress lining

You can easily line the body of a collarless dress (but not the sleeves) as follows:

1. Seam the shoulders, side seams, and any front or back garment seams. Insert the zipper if the pattern requires one.

2. Serge-seam the lining shoulder seams, side seams, and any front seam. Finish the back seam for a zipper as shown in Fig. 6-25. Serge-finish the lower lining edge 1" shorter than the finished dress hemline.

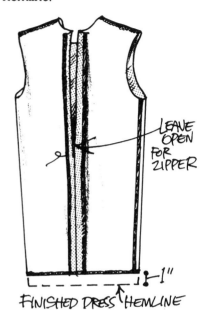

Fig. 6-25 Treat the dress lining and fabric as one layer when applying the neckline and sleeves.

3. With the lining and garment wrong sides together, machine- or serge-baste the neckline and armscye edges.

4. Treating the edge as a single layer, complete the neckline using any circular neckline finish from Chapter 4.

5. Set in the garment sleeves by straight-stitching and serge-finishing the seam allowances together.

6. Blind-stitch the lining to the zipper closure by hand and complete the garment according to the pattern instructions.

Free-hanging skirt lining

Lining a pull-on skirt—Simply seam both the skirt and the lining and serge-finish the lower lining edge 1" shorter than the finished skirt hemline. Place the skirt and lining wrong sides together and serge-finish the upper edge through both layers. Then, treating the upper edge as a single layer, complete the skirt according to pattern instructions or by using any pull-on waistband technique featured in Chapter 7.

Lining a skirt with a constructed waistband:

1. Sew darts or pleats and seam the skirt. Insert the zipper.

2. Serge the lining side seams and serge-finish the back seam allowances, vent, and lower edge (1" shorter than the finished skirt hemline). (Fig. 6-26)

> When serging the vent, round the lower corners so the lining won't show from the right side.

3. Slip the lining over the skirt, wrong sides together. Pleat the lining waistline to fit the skirt and serge- or machine-baste the waistline edges together.

4. Attach the waistband following pattern instructions or directions in Chapter 7. Blind-stitch the lining to the zipper tape by hand.

5. Complete the skirt following the pattern instructions.

Free-hanging pants lining

Use either of the previous skirt-lining methods to line pants, except cut the lower lining edges longer and hem them to the wrong side (by serge-finishing, turning, and top-stitching) to add weight and help hold the lining down.

Easy jacket lining

Fully line a jacket using this simple serger application:

1. Construct the body of the jacket, except for the upper collar and facing. Complete and set in the sleeves. Seam the upper collar to the facings. Press up the sleeve and jacket hems.

2. Serge-finish the bottom 3" of the facing where it will be exposed between the lining hem and the lower jacket edge. (Fig. 6-27)

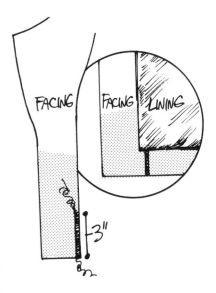

3. Serge-seam the lining body and set in the sleeves.

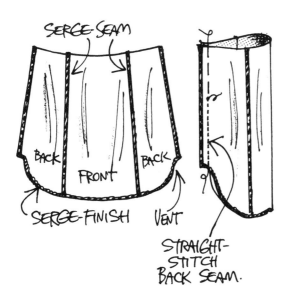

Fig. 6-26 Prepare the lining and baste it to the waistline edge.

4. With right sides together, serge-seam the lining to the facing, angling on and off the seam allowances 6" from the bottom edges. (Fig. 6-28)

Fig. 6-28 Serge-seam the lining to the facings.

5. Matching the cut edges, straight-stitch the upper collar and facing to the under collar and jacket.

6. With right sides together, serge-seam the lower edge of the jacket sleeve to the lining sleeve, being careful the lining is not twisted and aligned incorrectly. (Fig. 6-29)

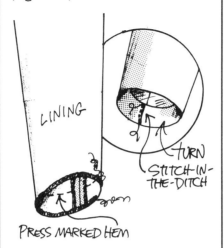

Fig. 6-29 Serge-seam the sleeve hem edge to the lining.

7. Turn the jacket right side out. Fold up the sleeve hems and stitch-in-the-ditch of the hem seamlines to secure.

8. Complete the jacket according to pattern instructions, including adding shoulder pads, tacking the lining to the garment at the shoulder and armscyes, and hemming.

NOTES

CHAPTER 7

SERGED WAISTLINE FINISHES

Serged Waistline Finishes

Pull-on Waistbands ✄ Constructed Waistbands ✄ Other Waistline Finishes

Pull-on Waistbands

The wearing comfort and construction ease of pull-on elastic waistbands make them a favorite, especially on today's wide variety of knit fabrics.

Choosing the elastic

Deciding which type of elastic to use for your garment can be confusing (see chart, next page). Many excellent types are now available, including some which recover well after being top-stitched through. Others are designed for specialty applications or for specific types of garments. (Fig. 7-1)

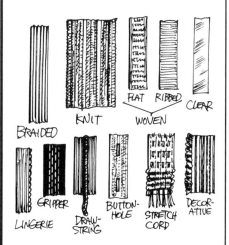

Fig. 7-1 Decide how to apply the elastic based on the type you choose.

Specialty elastics can often be serged onto the fabric instead of being straight-stitched, as called for in the manufacturer's instructions that accompany the elastic. You can easily apply most types by substituting the techniques in this chapter for traditional sewing methods.

General elastic pointers:

✄ Use the widest, longest, balanced 3-thread stitch when serging elastic to the garment so the elastic can recover to its original length most easily.

✄ Serge-seam through elastic with the elastic on top, stretching it to fit as you sew over it.

✄ When top-stitching over elastic, use a long stitch and stretch firmly or use a twin-needle.

✄ For added stretchability, top-stitch using elastic thread in the bobbin.

✄ After you've finished serging or top-stitching the elastic, steam it well (without touching it with the iron) to shrink it back to its original length.

✄ When the elastic is enclosed in a casing without being stitched through, make the casing 1/8" wider than the elastic so that the elastic can slip through easily but won't roll inside.

✄ When the elastic is loose in a casing, distribute the gathers evenly and stitch-in-the-ditch of the original seamlines to secure the elastic and prevent it from rolling. (Fig. 7-2)

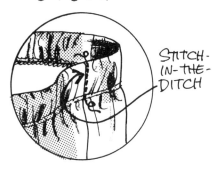

Fig. 7-2 Top-stitch vertically to keep the elastic from rolling and keep the gathering distributed evenly.

✄ With braided elastic, a 3/8" width or wider has more elasticity and recovery when serged to the fabric edge. The 1/8" width can be flatlocked (or zigzagged) over to gather anywhere on the fabric.

✄ When serging most elastics, be careful not to cut the edge with the knives. Only transparent elastic doesn't lose its stretch when nicked.

✄ For convenience, keep several types and widths of elastic on hand. Label each before storing or attach the manufacturer's instructions if available.

Elastic Selection Guidelines

Type	Most Common Widths	Characteristics	Common Uses	Serge Through	Top-stitch Through Center	In Casing
Braided	1/8", 1/4", 3/8", 1/2", 3/4", 1"	Mediumweight; narrows when stretched	General; all fabric weights; swimwear	Along edge only	No	Yes
Knit (including sport elastic)	1-1/4", 1-1/2", 2"	Mediumweight; less stretch than braided; maintains width when stretched	General; all fabric weights; pull-on waistbands	Yes	Yes	Yes
Woven	Flat: 1/2", 3/4", 1" Ribbed: 1", 1-1/4", 1-1/2", 2"	Heavier weight; usually flat nonroll or ribbed; less stretch than braided; maintains width when stretched	Flat for lightweight fabrics; ribbed for heavier fabrics	Along edge only	Along edge	Yes
Clear	1/4", 3/8", 1/2", 3/4"	Soft; lightweight; excellent stretch and recovery; narrows when stretched; not weakened by cutting	Light- to mediumweight fabric, swimwear and aerobicwear; stabilizing seams and edges	Yes	Yes	No (must stitch through to prevent rolling)
Lingerie	1/4", 1/2", 3/4", 1"	Soft; lightweight; may have plush or felt back; may have one picot edge	Lingerie	Along edge only (flat-locked)	Along edge	No
Gripper	1"	Lightweight; exposed spandex or rubber on one side	Cycling garments—usually to keep legs from riding up	Along edge only	Along edge	No
Drawstring	3/4", 1-1/4", 2"	Knit with drawcord down center—pulled to tighten after application	Activewear	Along edge only	Along edge	Yes
Buttonhole	3/4"	Knit with buttonholes 1" apart down center to change elastic length	Maternity; infants; children	No	Along edge	Yes
Stretch cord (Stitch 'n Stretch)	1", 1-1/2", 2-1/4"	Woven with spandex cords; applied flat and drawn up to gather	Light- to mediumweight fabrics; cuffs; waistlines	No	Yes	Yes (only after top-stitching through it)
Decorative	3"	Wide knit; strong; often with one ruffled edge; worn exposed—stitched to waistline edge	Waistbands	Along edge only	Along edge	No

When choosing which type and width of elastic to use for your garment, refer to the pattern envelope, the chart on page 81, and the information in this chapter. Through experience, you will find that elastic quality varies widely. When in doubt, ask for recommendations at your local fabric store or select a name brand for the best performance.

Measuring elastic—Although most patterns include elastic measurement specifications, keep these general guidelines in mind:

✂ When unsure of the length needed, fit the elastic comfortably to the body and add 1/2" for seaming.

✂ Because elastic stretch varies, be sure the length you are using for a pants pattern will fit over the widest part of your hips.

✂ If you're having trouble serge-seaming elastic to stretchy or slippery fabrics such as nylon/ *Lycra* or lingerie knits, machine-baste vertically across the elastic first to hold it in position. (Fig. 7-3)

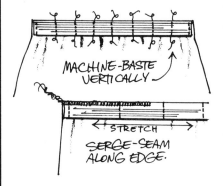

Fig. 7-3 Control difficult applications by machine-basting before serge-seaming.

✂ Even though sew-through elastics can be steamed to shrink them back to shape, cut them a little shorter because some recovery will be lost.

✂ More elastic stretch is usually required to control heavier fabrics, so cut the elastic a little shorter.

✂ Softer elastic usually has more stretch, so cut it a little shorter.

Pull-on waistband types

Most pull-on waistbands are much easier to apply with the serger than with the conventional sewing machine because no trimming is required and serged stitching stretches automatically with the elastic. Use a knit elastic for best results. When you'll be top-stitching through the elastic, use a sport elastic (designed to be stitched through without stretching out of shape).

Many techniques and variations of techniques are taught by serger professionals for applying pull-on waistbands. Try several to see which is easiest for you.

Wrapped and top-stitched— The simple pull-on waistband application on page 7 is one of the easiest. The circular edge is serge-finished and top-stitched over the circular-stitched elastic to form a casing. After the gathers are distributed evenly, it is stitched-in-the-ditch (see Fig. 7-2) to maintain the distribution and prevent the elastic from twisting in the casing.

For a flat front on this waistband treatment, first distribute the gathers evenly and stitch-in-the-ditch at the center back and side seams only. On the front, ease out most of the fullness for 2-1/2" to 3" on either side of the center-front seam. Stitch vertically through the waistband to position all the gathering at the sides. (Fig. 7-4)

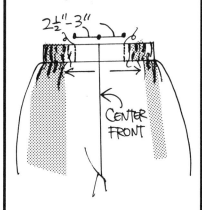

Fig. 7-4 For a flattering flat front, push all the gathering to the sides and straight-stitch through the casing.

Serged, turned, and top-stitched—For another easy pull-on waistband, serge the elastic to the wrong side of the fabric, turn the edge to the wrong side, and top-stitch through the bottom of the elastic to secure.

1. Cut out the garment with the waistline seam allowance double the width of the elastic.

2. Seam the garment together.

3. Fit the elastic comfortably around your waist (usually stretching it at least 2" more than the actual measurement). Cut the elastic 1/2" longer than the desired length, overlap the ends, and sew them together forming a circle.

4. Quartermark the waistline edge and the elastic. (Fig. 7-5)

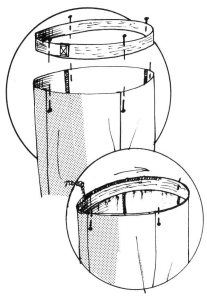

Fig. 7-5 Matching quartermarks, serge-seam the elastic to the waistline edge.

> **When you're working on difficult fabric or if you're having trouble aligning the edges between the quartermarks, divide both circles into eighths instead.**

5. Place the elastic against the wrong side of the waistline edge, matching the quartermarks. Serge-seam, overlapping the stitching.

6. Turn the elastic to the wrong side and top-stitch along the lower edge to secure it, stretching as you sew. (Fig. 7-6)

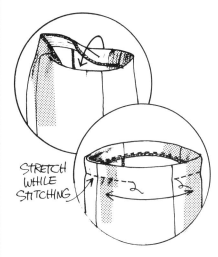

Fig. 7-6 Fold the elastic under and top-stitch.

7. Stitch-in-the-ditch of the vertical seamlines to secure the elastic.

> **The serged, turned, and top-stitched technique is also used to apply braided or clear elastic on swimwear.**

There are several common variations of serged, turned, and top-stitched waistbands:

✄ To hold the elastic firmly in place while turning and during wearing, straight-stitch along the unattached elastic edge before turning. Use a long stitch and

stretch the elastic as you sew over it. (Fig. 7-7)

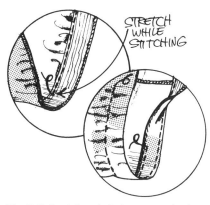

Fig. 7-7 Straight-stitch the unattached edge before turning and top-stitching.

✄ After serge-seaming sew-through sport elastic to the edge, folding, and top-stitching, top-stitch additional equidistant rows through all layers, stretching the elastic as you sew. (Fig. 7-8)

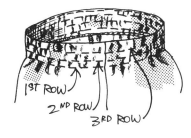

Fig. 7-8 Top-stitch additional rows through all layers.

✄ To ensure stretchability when top-stitching through the elastic, use a twin-needle or a narrow zigzag. (Fig. 7-9)

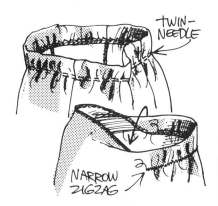

Fig. 7-9 Increase stretchability by top-stitching with a stretch stitch.

Sport elastic with stitching lines—Several brands of sew-through sport elastic have no stitching lines and are best applied by the serged, turned, and top-stitched method described previously. On other brands, you'll see stitching lines between the knitted sections. On light- or medium-weight fabrics, use your serger to apply this type of sport elastic quickly:

1. Cut out the garment with the waistline seam allowance equal to the elastic width plus 1/2". Cut the elastic 3" to 5" smaller than your waistline measurement because it will stretch some when it is sewn through.

2. Overlap the elastic ends and zigzag them together. Seam the garment. Quartermark both.

3. Position the elastic on the right side of the waistline edge, matching the quartermarks. Serge-seam the waistline edge.

4. Turn the elastic to the wrong side only the width of the seam allowance (you'll leave the elastic exposed so you can see the stitching lines). (Fig. 7-10)

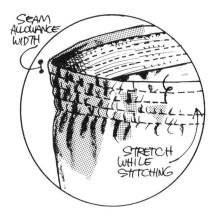

Fig. 7-10 Leave sport elastic exposed if it has stitching lines.

5. Beginning at the bottom row, straight-stitch along the lines, stretching the elastic to fit the fabric.

One-step banded casing—Serge this quick pull-on waistline in one step without having to turn and straight-stitch to complete it. The technique may take a little practice and is usually best on easy-to-sew fabrics.

1. Cut out the garment with a waistline allowance twice the elastic width plus 1-1/4".

2. Press an amount equal to twice the elastic width plus 1" to the right side 1/4" above the waistline and then press half back again so the raw edge meets the first fold. This will be the waistband casing. (Fig. 7-11)

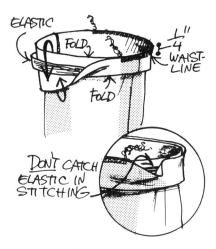

Fig. 7-11 Fold back a casing at the top of the garment. Insert the elastic as you serge-seam around the edge.

3. Fit the elastic to your waistline and zigzag it into a circle.

4. Place a section of the elastic between the two sections of the casing and begin serging the edge, being careful not to catch the elastic in the serging. Manipulate the fabric so you are always serging over a flat section as you complete the circle. Overlap the ends of the serging.

5. Distribute the fullness evenly and stitch-in-the-ditch across the elastic to secure.

This technique also can be used when the casing is a separate band. Cut the band twice the elastic width plus 1" and leave a 1/4" seam allowance at the garment waistline. Serge-seam in a circle with the band wrong sides together against the right side of the waistline edge and the elastic sandwiched inside the band. (Fig. 7-12)

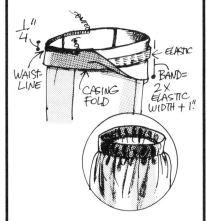

Fig. 7-12 Apply a separate casing in the same manner (see Fig. 7-11), gradually sandwiching the elastic inside the band as you serge-seam the edges next to it.

Threaded—If you are unsure of the elastic fit (or when the pattern calls for pulling through a drawstring), you may choose to complete the casing before applying the elastic, instead of using any of the previous techniques. Cut out the garment with a waistline allowance twice the elastic width plus 1/4". Serge-finish, turn, and top-stitch the casing first, leaving an opening for the elastic. Thread the elastic through, lap the ends, and zigzag them together. Straight-stitch the opening closed and stitch-in-the-ditch or top-stitch to secure the elastic. (Fig. 7-13)

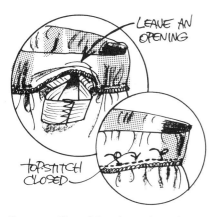

Fig. 7-13 Thread the elastic through a casing for a sure fit.

Covered and serge-seamed—If you're a one-step-at-a-time person, you may find it easier to cover and complete the waistband before applying it to the garment. (Fig. 7-14)

1. Cut a band the same circumference as the garment waistline plus 1/2" (for seam allowances) by twice the elastic width plus 1".

2. Fit sew-through sport elastic comfortably around your waist and add 1/2" for seam allowances. Lap and zigzag the ends to form a circle.

3. Serge-seam the band into a circle and fold it wrong sides together. Sandwich the elastic inside the band and straight-stitch the lower edge just below it.

4. Stretch and release the band to distribute the fullness evenly, pinning to hold it temporarily in place.

5. Beginning at the bottom of the elastic and stretching as you stitch, top-stitch parallel rows around the band. Use the width of the presser foot as an easy width guide.

6. If necessary, trim the waistline seam allowance to 1/4". Position the band right sides together against the garment waistline with the seam at the left sideseam and the band on top. Stretch and pin to align it. Serge-seam in a circle.

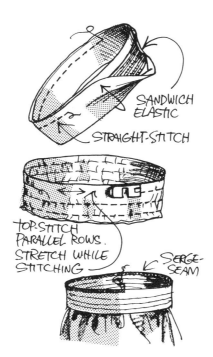

Fig. 7-14 If you prefer, cover a waistband before serge-seaming it to the garment.

Constructed Waistbands

Although pull-on waistbands are easy and comfortable, there are times when your garment styling calls for a rigid constructed waistband that is interfaced and completed before applying. Use the serger to speed up the sewing process.

Before attaching a constructed waistband, you will need to complete the garment (with the possible exception of the hem) and apply a zipper or a placket as specified in your pattern.

Basic serged waistband

1. Serge-finish the long unnotched edge of the interfaced waistband with the needle on the seamline. Position the other side of the waistband right sides together against the garment waistline, matching the markings for side seams, center back, and overlaps. Serge-seam. (Fig. 7-15)

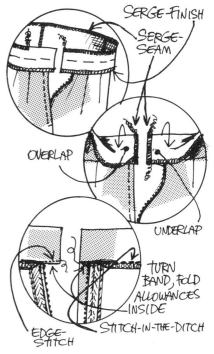

Fig. 7-15 Use serger techniques to apply a basic constructed waistband.

2. Fold the band right sides together, turn up the serge-finished edge on the overlap, and serge-seam the ends.

3. Turn the band right side out and press. Tuck the waistband allowances into the underlap, angling the serge-finished edge of the underlap over the top of the zipper.

4. Stitch-in-the-ditch from the right side and edge-stitch the underlap closed.

Clean-finished method—For a flatter finish on the inside of the garment, turn the serge-finished waistband edge to the wrong side and press before applying it to the garment. Serge-seam the overlap end but not the underlap before turning in step 3. Press the bottom edge of the underlap seam allowances to the inside. Turn and top-stitch through all layers near the edge for the length of the band, then serge-finish the end of the underlap. (Fig. 7-16)

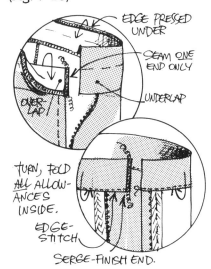

Fig. 7-16 For a clean finish, turn the inside waistband edge under and edge-stitch through all layers.

Elastic inset method—Before applying a 1-1/4"-wide constructed waistband, mark a line 2-1/4" on either side of the side seams on the wrong side of the underband. (Fig. 7-17) (This is easiest using a disappearing marker on the band interfacing.) Cut two 4" pieces of 1"-wide elastic and straight-stitch 1/2" from the ends over the markings, centering the elastic at the side seams. Straight-stitch horizontally through the center of the elastic, stretching it to fit the fabric. Complete the waistband as outlined in the numbered steps above.

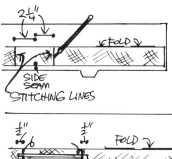

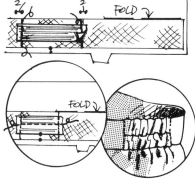

Fig. 7-17 Draw stitching lines on the interfacing next to both side seams. Straight-stitch elastic over the lines and then again horizontally before applying the waistband.

Lightweight application

On light- to medium-weight fabrics, you may choose to serge-seam the waistband through all layers when applying it.

1. Fold the waistband right sides together and serge-seam the ends. On the underlap, straight-stitch the seamline from the end to the dot marking. (Fig. 7-18)

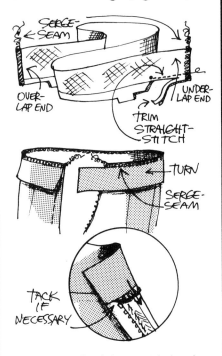

Fig. 7-18 Finish a lighter-weight band before serge-seaming both layers at once to the waistline.

2. Trim the lower edge of the underlap, angling away from the end at the dot.

3. Turn the waistband right side out and press. Serge-seam it to the waistline, matching the markings.

4. Press the waistband into position with the seam allowance toward the garment. If the serged allowance is visible on the right side edges, hide it by hand-tacking at the edges.

Other Waistline Finishes

Some garments other than pants and skirts also call for a waistline finish—dresses, jumpsuits, jumpers, and some longer tops. The pattern may have separate top and bottom pieces, or it may be cut all in one.

No-seam waistline

When a dress or top is cut in one piece without a waistline seam, a waistline can be applied by zigzagging or flatlocking over narrow braided elastic from the wrong side without stitching through it. Then adjust it to fit and sew the ends together. You may flatlock over clear elastic instead, but you must stretch it to fit and stitch through it to keep it from rolling. The no-seam waistline application is not the strongest option, but it will work on lightweight and delicate garments. (Fig. 7-19)

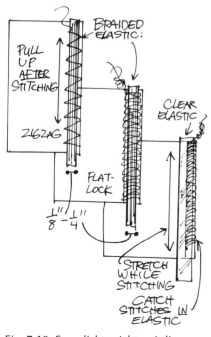

Fig. 7-19 For a lightweight waistline treatment, sew or serge over narrow elastic.

For more control at the waistline, add a casing with elastic or a drawstring. Use a lining fabric or comparable material. With your serger, simultaneously cut and finish one side of the casing. Serge-finish the other long edge (or cut with a selvage along the second edge). Cut the strip the elastic width plus 5/8" by the garment waistline measurement plus 1". (Fig. 7-20) Press under 1/2" on both short ends and straight-stitch the casing to the inside of the garment at the waistline position along the serging needlelines on both edges, butting the folded ends but leaving them open to thread the elastic.

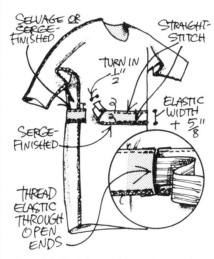

Fig. 7-20 Straight-stitch a casing on the wrong side of the waistline, leaving the folded ends open for threading elastic.

If you choose to use a drawstring instead of elastic, make two buttonholes 1" apart at the center front before applying the casing on the underside, folding over and overlapping one casing end. Thread the drawstring through the buttonholes. (Fig. 7-21)

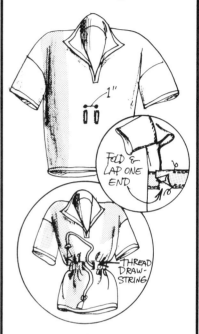

Fig. 7-21 For a drawstring, sew buttonholes at the center front before applying a casing.

Seamed waistline

Although you can serge-seam the waistline, on many garments you will want a seam allowance wider than the serged stitch. Then straight-stitch the seamline and serge-finish the allowances together. With either method, the waistline seam will often need to be reinforced (see page 30).

With narrow elastic casing— To easily build more stretchability into the waistline seam, straight-stitch on the 5/8" seamline and serge-finish the allowances together (without trimming) to form a casing. Leave an opening for threading. Thread 3/8" elastic through the casing, fit it comfortably to your waist, and sew the ends together. Serge the opening closed, overlapping the stitching on both sides. (Fig. 7-22)

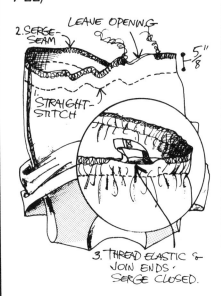

Fig. 7-22 Make a quick narrow elastic casing inside the waistline seam allowances.

With wide elastic—Cut out the garment with waistline seam allowances the width of the elastic.

1. Straight-stitch the waistline, right sides together, on the seamline. Open up the seam.

2. Fit the elastic comfortably around your waist and zigzag it into a circle. Quartermark both the elastic and the waistline.

3. Place the elastic between the allowances against the seam allowance of the bottom section, match the marks, and serge-seam. (Fig. 7-23)

4. Trim the allowance of the top garment section to 1/4". Pull the garment flat. Fold the elastic toward the top section, and top-stitch the upper edge in place from the right side, stretching as you sew.

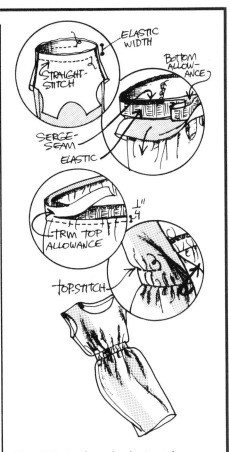

Fig. 7-23 Apply wide elastic at the waistline by serging it to one allowance, trimming the other allowance, and top-stitching. Stretch while stitching the elastic.

CHAPTER 8

SERGED CLOSURES

Serged Closures

Serged Zippers ✄ Elastic Button Loops ✄ Other Closure Options

Serged Zippers

Although the serger can be used to duplicate a hand-picked zipper, the process is difficult and time-consuming. In this book, we will focus only on faster and easier techniques and recommend the conventional sewing-machine methods for other simple zipper applications.

Clean-finished

You can easily use your serger for two zipper techniques in which all of the serging is hidden on the inside of the garment:

With exposed zipper teeth— Use this easy method when both ends of the zipper will be crossed and secured by an intersecting seam. This is a good technique for pockets or a sporty closure and uses 1/4" seam allowances. (Fig. 8-1)

1. Align the right side of one fabric edge with the right-side edge of the zipper tape, positioning the zipper pull at least 2" past the end of the fabric.

2. Serge-seam with the zipper on top, placing the needle close to the zipper teeth. Use the widest balanced stitch on your machine and hold both layers taut so the presser foot won't slip off the zipper teeth.

3. Repeat steps 1 and 2 for the opposite edge, aligning the second fabric with the first.

4. After pressing the seam allowances toward the fabric, top-stitch along the fabric edge, through all layers, if desired.

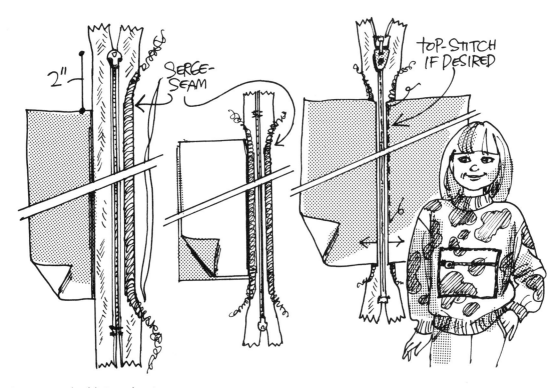

Fig. 8-1 Serge-seam the fabric to the zipper tape.

To secure the zipper ends, pull the zipper tab down, and bar-tack above and below it using a wide zigzag or hand-stitch. Sew the top end together for a joined application, or unzip and stitch both sides for a separating closure. (Fig. 8-2)

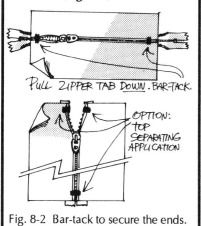

PULL ZIPPER TAB DOWN. BAR-TACK.

OPTION:
TOP
SEPARATING
APPLICATION

Fig. 8-2 Bar-tack to secure the ends.

With the zipper applied to a finished seam — (Use this application for a conventional centered zipper):

1. Sew the seam using the serge-finished and straight-stitched method on page 24.

2. Place the right side of the zipper in position against the pressed-open seam allowances. Temporarily secure the long edges with transparent tape. (Fig. 8-3)

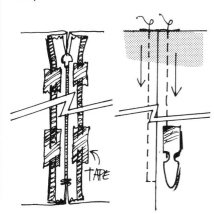

TAPE

Fig. 8-3 Tape the zipper into position on the wrong side. Top-stitch from the right side.

3. From the right side, mark and top-stitch around the placket as you would conventionally. Remove the tape.

For a separating zipper, complete the garment first and top-stitch the edges over it. (Fig. 8-4)

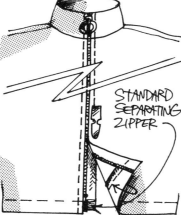

STANDARD
SEPARATING
ZIPPER

Fig. 8-4 Turn up the hem and finish the neckline before applying a separating zipper.

To fit a longer separating zipper, cut off from the upper end of the zipper (rather than the lower end) so the separating closure remains intact.

Decoratively serge-finished and top-stitched

When you choose to display decorative serging on the right side of the garment, the zipper application is easy. Decoratively serge-finish both fabric edges and simply top-stitch them over the right side of the tape on a decorative zipper, butting them next to the teeth. (Fig. 8-5)

DECORATIVE
ZIPPER

TOP-
STITCH

Fig. 8-5 Lap and top-stitch decorative edges over the zipper tape.

On lightweight fabrics, serge over a folded edge for more stability. (See Fig. 10-4)

Try these decorative zipper variations, too:

With one clean-finished edge and one lapped decorative edge:

1. Place the zipper face down on the right side of one seamline edge with the closure extending at least 2".

2. Using a medium-width, medium-length, balanced stitch, serge-seam the zipper tape to the fabric without trimming the tape. Hold both layers taut so the presser foot won't slip off the zipper teeth. (Fig. 8-6)

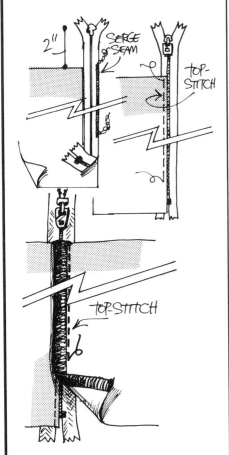

Fig. 8-6 For a decorative lapped zipper, clean-finish one side before top-stitching the other.

3. Fold the fabric to the right side close to the zipper teeth and top-stitch along the fold.

4. Finish the opposite edge using any of the decorative edge-finishing methods in Chapter 10.

5. Lap the decorative edge over the zipper teeth and top-stitch it in place on the unstitched side of the zipper.

With the zipper applied to a placket:

1. Cut a placket opening, angling the last 1/2" to the lower corners. (Fig. 8-7)

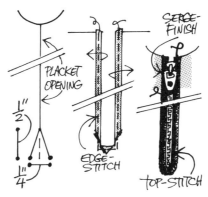

Fig. 8-7 Cut, edge-stitch, and decoratively serge-finish a placket before lapping and top-stitching it over a zipper.

2. Press the edges to the wrong side and edge-stitch to anchor them in place.

3. Using a short, narrow, balanced stitch with decorative thread in the upper looper, serge-finish the placket edge. At the point, pull the fabric out straight in front of the foot as you serge over it. (See Fig. 3-34)

4. Lap the placket over the zipper, butting the serge-finished edges to the zipper teeth. Top-stitch around the edge on the serging needleline.

With the zipper applied to a circular opening:

1. Cut a slit in the fabric with angled corners at the last 1/2" of both ends.

2. Fold, top-stitch, and serge-finish the edges following the instructions in the previous steps 2 and 3. Overlap the serging ends for several stitches, beginning and ending by clearing the stitch finger. Hide the thread tails on the underside. (Fig. 8-8)

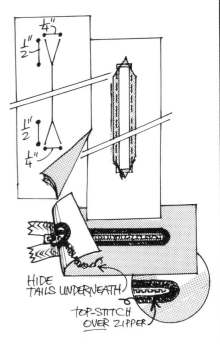

Fig. 8-8 Overlap the decorative serging after cutting and edge-stitching a circular placket.

3. Lap the placket over the zipper and top-stitch around all edges.

Elastic Button Loops

When choosing the closure for a garment, consider using elastic thread or cording for several simple serger techniques.

Serged elastic button loops

For a simple closure on formal wear, baby garments, or casual sportswear, serge-finish the edge using mediumweight elastic thread in the lower looper. The result is delicate and feminine but also quite durable. Use one of two methods:

With decorative stitching:

1. Using decorative thread in the upper looper and a short, medium- to wide-width, balanced 3-thread stitch, serge-finish one closure edge from the right side. Adjust the tension so the elastic thread is entirely hidden on the underside.

> You will probably need to test and adjust to perfect this stitching because elastic thread is very stretchy and characteristics vary from brand to brand.

2. Use a fine crochet hook or tapestry needle to pull out loops of the lower looper (elastic) thread at regular intervals. This will slightly narrow the stitch and anchor the loops. (Fig. 8-9)

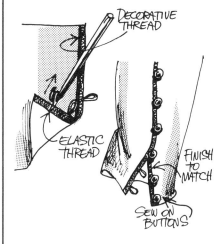

Fig. 8-9 Serge easy button loops using elastic thread in the lower looper.

3. Serge-finish the opposite edge to match.

4. Sew buttons along the serged edge, opposite the loops.

> If the serged stitch is not significantly narrowed or changed when the loops are pulled, serge-finish the opposite edge with the same thread and settings. If the stitch does narrow, change to serger or all-purpose thread in the lower looper and adjust for a stitch width to match the other edge.

With a clean-finished edge:

1. Use serger or all-purpose thread in the needle and upper looper, mediumweight elastic thread in the lower looper, and a short, medium- to wide-width, balanced 3-thread stitch. Serge the edge from the wrong side with the needle on the seamline.

2. Pull the elastic loops toward the garment. (Fig. 8-10)

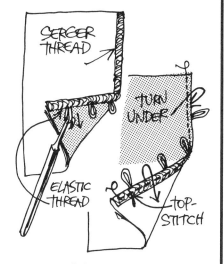

Fig. 8-10 Pull the loops toward the garment and top-stitch the serging to the underside.

3. Turn the serge-finishing to the underside and top-stitch it in place.

Serge-covered cording

Make custom-colored elastic cording or heavier elastic thread using a rolled-edge stitch and the filler-cord technique (see Fig. 4-3). For the best coverage, use woolly nylon in the upper looper. Do NOT stretch the cord when serging over it. Use the serge-covered cording for single or multiple button loops. (Fig. 8-11)

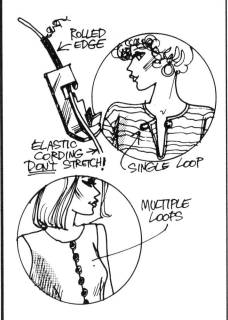

Fig. 8-11 Serge over elastic cording to custom color it for single or multiple button loops.

Make a decorative button loop for a larger button by braiding several strands of serge-covered cording. Secure the ends by straight-stitching over them. Hide them in a seam or sew a matching button over them. (Fig. 8-12)

Fig. 8-12 Braid serge-covered cording for large decorative button loops.

Serge over covered cording

Use the technique described above to make serge-covered cording to use as a filler cord under a wider serged stitch.

1. Decoratively serge-finish the edge over a strand of serge-covered cording, leaving generous cording tails on both ends. Chain off without stitching through the cording. (See Fig. 6-7)

2. Starting in the center, pull out button loops using a fine crochet hook or tapestry needle. The cording will move freely under the decorative serging, so hold the previous loop in position as you pull more cording from the loose tail. (Fig. 8-13)

3. Anchor the filler cord by edge-stitching, catching the ends of the loops.

As with the clean-finished elastic loop technique (page 43), you can hide the serged edge on the underside. Serge from the right side because the elastic cording is under the upper looper thread. Pull the loops toward the garment, instead of away from it, before turning the serge-finished edge to the underside and top-stitching. (See Fig. 8-10)

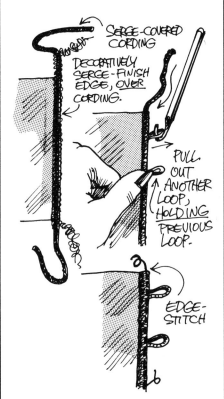

Fig. 8-13 Beginning in the center, pull loops of elastic out at the edge. Edge-stitch to secure.

Other Closure Options

For the quickest serged garments, choose pullover tops and pull-on bottoms, which don't have closures. But when your pattern or styling calls for a closure, you can use the serger to enhance several other traditional closure techniques:

✄ Decoratively serge-finish the lips of a two-piece bound buttonhole before top-stitching them in place. (Fig. 8-14)

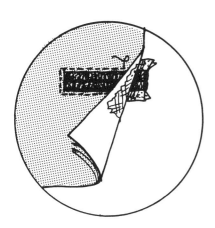

Fig. 8-14 Use decorative serging to highlight a two-piece bound buttonhole.

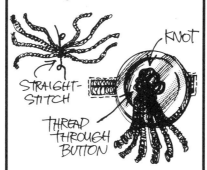

Fig. 8-15 Use strands of serged thread chain for a novel button attachment.

✄ Apply *Velcro* by decoratively serge-seaming one edge to the fabric with wrong sides of the garment and *Velcro* together. Straight-stitch the other long edge in place. (Fig. 8-16)

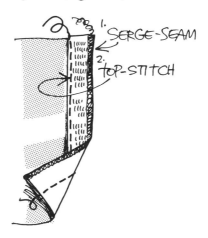

Fig. 8-16 Decoratively serge-seam *Velcro* to the fabric edge.

✄ Construct cording loops for a decorative closure treatment. Serge and turn cording following the instructions for spaghetti straps on page 129. Use the cording for single button loops or multiple button loops, or tie it into frogs.

✄ Use serged thread chain for the eye of a hook and eye. Apply it following the techniques on page 126 for a thread-chain belt loop.

NOTES

CHAPTER 9

SERGED POCKETS

Serged Pockets

Patch Pockets ✀ Inside Pockets

Patch Pockets

Make functional patch pockets in a wide variety of shapes, sizes, and styles, using speedy serger techniques. Complete the pockets first before attaching them (usually by top-stitching) to the garment.

> **Because the upper corners will receive the most stress, reinforce them by back-stitching or sewing small triangles. Use a patch of fusible interfacing on the under-side of the garment for added strength or if the fabric is delicate or loosely woven. (Fig. 9-1)**

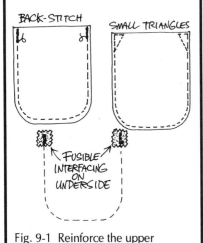

Fig. 9-1 Reinforce the upper corners when top-stitching patch pockets to the garment.

Consider these options before deciding how to construct patch pockets:

✀ To finish the pockets before applying them, either decoratively serge-finish the outer edge, turn the edges under evenly, or line the pocket, enclosing the seams between the pocket and the lining. (Fig. 9-2)

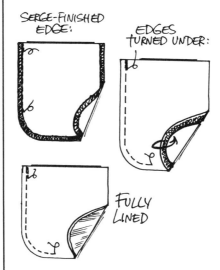

Fig. 9-2 Complete the pockets before applying them.

> **When turning the pocket edges under, serge-finish around the curved lower edges with the needle positioned on the line where the edge will be turned. On the curves tighten the needle tension (see page 66) or set the differential feed at 1.5 or 2.0 to help ease the seam allowance when it is turned under. (Fig. 9-3)**

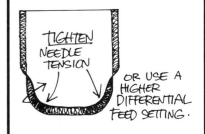

Fig. 9-3 Use gathering methods from Chapter 6 to ease rounded corners before turning them under.

✀ Patch pockets are most often square or rounded but can be any shape. For the fastest serged construction, round the lower corners (if they aren't already) so the sides and bottom edge can be serged continuously.

When serge-finishing the outer edges of a pocket using a satin-length decorative stitch, narrow the stitch width to help negotiate around the lower corners more easily. Also stay-stitch just inside the serger needleline as a handy stitching guideline and also to keep the fabric from stretching as it is serged over. (Fig. 9-4)

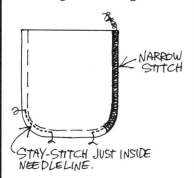

Fig. 9-4 Make perfectly rounded corners when decoratively serging the edge.

✂ Choose to finish the top of pockets with a turned hem, decorative serge-finishing, or lining. (Fig. 9-5)

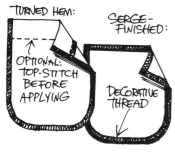

Fig. 9-5 Finish the top of the pocket in a way that complements the garment and the fabric.

To turn back a hem on an unlined pocket when the other edges will be turned under:

1. Serge-finish the hem edge.

2. Fold the hem to the right side along the hemline and serge-finish the sides and lower edges. (Fig. 9-6)

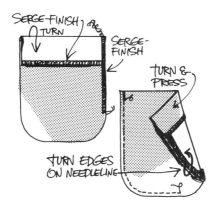

Fig. 9-6 Serge a clean-finished pocket quickly and easily.

When serge-finishing the edges of a pocket with square corners that will be turned under, serge the lower edge first and press, wrapping it toward the front of the pocket before serging the sides. This will make it much easier to turn the corners squarely. (Fig. 9-7)

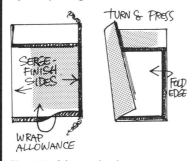

Fig. 9-7 If the pocket has square corners, wrap the lower allowance toward the pocket before serging the sides.

3. Turn the hem back to the underside of the pocket, work the upper corners into sharp points, and press carefully, turning the remainder of the edge to the underside along the serged needleline.

For a decorative finish on fabrics with no discernible right or wrong side, serge-finish the hem edge from the wrong side using decorative thread and a short stitch length. Turn the hem to the right side and top-stitch it in place along the serging needleline. Then decoratively serge-finish the sides to match. (Fig. 9-8)

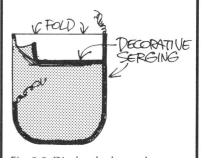

Fig. 9-8 Display the hem edge on the outside for a piped effect.

You have several options when lining a pocket (Fig. 9-9):

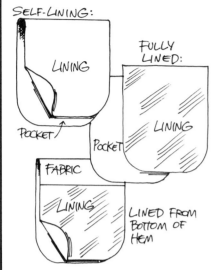

Fig. 9-9 When lining a pocket, decide which option to use.

Cut a self-lining—When the pocket fabric is light- or medium-weight, quickly line a pocket by cutting the pocket double with a fold at the top edge.

Fully line the pocket—Cut a separate lining piece the same size as the pocket. Then trim the lining about 1/8" smaller on all the cut edges so the garment fabric will wrap slightly to the underside when the pocket is turned.

When serge-seaming lining to the fabric on both sides of a square corner, wrap the allowances by serge-seaming one edge and pressing it toward the pocket before you serge-seam the adjoining edge. (See Fig. 9-10)

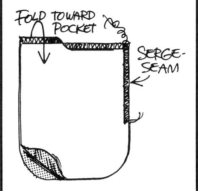

Fig. 9-10 Wrap any square corners on a lined pocket so they will turn neatly.

Line the pocket to the bottom of the hem—Cut a lining to extend from the bottom of the hem to the lower pocket edge. When cutting out, allow an additional 1/2" at the top edge for seam allowances.

A few more considerations:

✄ Interface pockets if the fabric is lightweight or loosely woven or the pocket is cut on the bias. Also interface to reinforce a pocket which will receive lots of wear and tear. When compatible with the fabric, use fusible interfacing for speed and ease of handling.

✄ Select from a wide range of decorative options, if desired. Apply any decorative treatment before the pocket is stitched to the garment. Use serged tucks or tuck variations (page 73), any decorative flatlocking stitch, or cut the pocket on the bias to accent a plaid or stripe. (Fig. 9-12)

When a lined pocket will have all of the serge-seaming enclosed on the inside, leave an opening on a straight edge in the least conspicuous place (depending on where the pocket will be positioned on the garment) for turning the pocket right side out. To maintain an even seam width, clear the stitch finger at the edge of the opening rather than serging on or off the fabric. When the pocket is turned (with the allowances pressed to the inside) and top-stitched in place, the opening will be closed without hand-stitching. (Fig. 9-11)

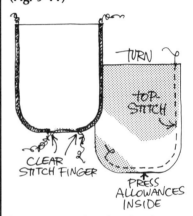

Fig. 9-11 On a lined pocket, leave an opening for turning in the least conspicuous place.

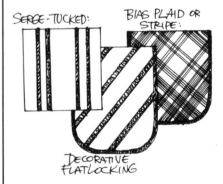

Fig. 9-12 Add decorative detailing to enhance any patch pocket.

Pocket flaps

Apply pocket flaps if the style dictates:

Self-flaps—Cut out the pocket with extra height equal to the depth of the flap. Use this technique on a self-lined pocket, for a single-layer pocket of reversible fabric or fabric with no discernible right or wrong side, or for a pocket with a hem wide enough to accommodate the additional flap depth. Decoratively serge-finish with a balanced stitch or top-stitch around the entire pocket rectangle edge on a fully lined pocket. Position the pocket on the garment with the flap up. Top-stitch again, ending at the flap foldline. Then fold down the flap. (Fig. 9-13)

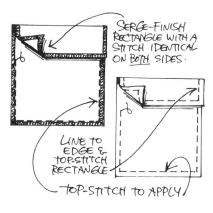

Fig. 9-13 Add a self-flap to a pocket by cutting it deeper and folding the top edge down.

Separate flaps—Construct a flap using the same techniques as you used for the corresponding pocket. For the quickest finish, leave the top edge unstitched. Serge-finish the top edge, fold and press the flap down, and straight-stitch the flap to the garment along the foldline. Top-stitch near the top of the flap to conceal the seam underneath.

If you prefer a flap without top-stitching, use the method for a fully lined pocket to construct the flap. Then fold, press, and straight-stitch the flap to the garment on the foldline and again close to the edge. (Fig. 9-14)

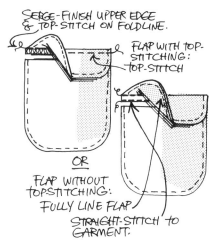

Fig. 9-14 Construct a separate flap and top-stitch it above the pocket.

> **Construct rectangular mock welt pockets using the method for separate flaps. Straight-stitch the flaps to the garment, turning them up instead of down. Top-stitch across the ends to secure. (Fig. 9-15)**
>
>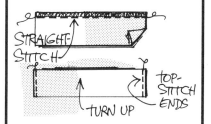
>
> Fig. 9-15 Apply a mock welt pocket after using the instructions for constructing a pocket flap.

Banded pocket

Trim the top of a patch pocket with a contrasting band of fabric. This technique is often used with ribbing to match a neckline, cuff, or waistline finish.

1. Cut the band the pocket width by two times the desired band depth plus 1/2" for seam allowances. Cut the pocket with an upper seam allowance of 1/4" and serge-finish the sides.

2. Fold the band in half lengthwise with wrong sides together, serge-seam the ends, and turn the band right side out.

3. With raw edges matching, center the band on top of the pocket, right sides together. Fold the seam allowances back over the band and serge-seam across the top of the pocket using a wide, medium-length, balanced stitch. (Fig. 9-16)

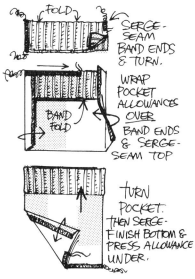

Fig. 9-16 Construct a pocket with a contrasting band at the top.

4. Serge-finish the bottom edge and press the band up. Turn and press the side and bottom seam allowances to the wrong side.

5. Position the pocket on the garment and fold it down, keeping the lower seam allowance in position. Straight-stitch along the seam creaseline. (Fig. 9-17)

Fig. 9-17 Straight-stitch the pocket bottom from the inside. Top-stitch the sides through all layers.

6. Fold the pocket up and top-stitch along both sides to secure.

If you prefer no top-stitching on the pocket (on a sweater fabric, for example), machine baste in step 6 and blind-stitch the pocket on by hand from the wrong side, using the basting as a guide.

Pleated pocket

Make easy pleated pockets for a full skirt or a jacket using a serge-finished rectangle. Simply mark pleats on the lower rectangle edge and top-stitch them into position for 1/2" to 1-1/2" before top-stitching the pocket to the garment. (Fig. 9-18)

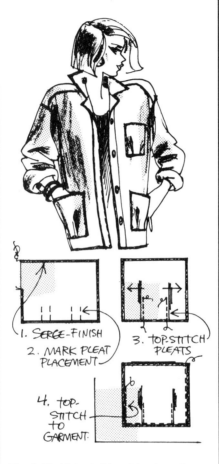

Fig. 9-18 Make fashionable pleated pockets in four easy steps.

Tulip pocket

For a youthful, whimsical look, make two-piece pockets that resemble tulips.

1. Cut two bias squares the height and width of the desired pocket.

2. Fold the squares diagonally, wrong sides together, and round two corners of each, using a cup or saucer as a guide. (Fig. 9-19)

Fig. 9-19 Create tulip pockets from two folded squares.

3. Decoratively serge-finish all of the outer edges and secure the ends. (See Fig. 9-4)

4. Layer the pieces across each other in position on the garment and top-stitch them in place.

For tulip pockets with no decorative serge-finishing, fold the squares right sides together. Serge-seam the curved edges, leaving an opening for turning as described in Fig. 9-11.

Double pocket

Quickly create a decorative double pocket with a self-flap:

1. Cut a rectangle the width of the pocket by five times the pocket depth. Fold the rectangle short ends together and round the top corners evenly.

2. On the folded end, fold again an amount equal to the pocket depth. (Fig. 9-20)

3. Using a short, narrow to medium-width, balanced stitch and decorative thread, serge continuously around the sides and curved end.

4. Top-stitch the pocket to the garment up to the folded open edge and press the curved end down to form the flap. You'll have one pocket behind the flap and one underneath it.

> **Vary the width of the decorative stitch depending on the weight of the fabric, making sure to catch both layers when serging.**
>
> **This pocket technique works best for lighter weight fabrics with which excess bulk will not be a concern.**

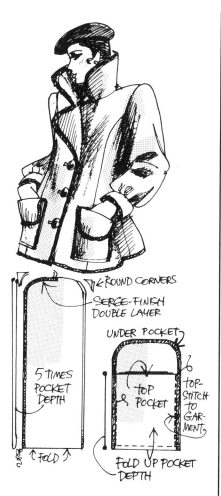

Fig. 9-20 Construct a double pocket with a self-flap using a long fabric rectangle.

Zipped pocket

Apply a zipper to an unlined pocket using any of the zipper installation techniques beginning on page 90. Simply cut out the pocket any desired shape or size and cut it apart anywhere you want a zipper. After applying the zipper, decoratively serge-finish all the pocket edges, following the instructions given previously, and top-stitch all edges of the pocket to the garment. (Fig. 9-21)

Fig. 9-21 Apply a zipper in any position on a pocket before finishing and top-stitching all edges to the garment.

> **Cut any serge-finished pocket with gradual curves or angles to ensure the most even stitching.**

Inside Pockets

Using the serger to seam and finish any type of inside pocket will save you the time of trimming and clipping necessary for traditional methods, and the results are both neat and durable.

Bottom inseam pocket

For an inseam pocket in a pair of pants or a skirt, follow these steps:

1. Serge-seam the pocket pieces to the side seams, right sides together, without trimming the edge.

> If the pocket opening is on the bias or the fabric is delicate or loosely woven, reinforce the seamline by serging over a lightweight stabilizer following the instructions on page 30.

2. Straight-stitch from the waistline to the top of the pocket opening and back-stitch to secure. Back-stitch and straight-stitch down from the bottom pocket opening for 3" to 4". (Fig. 9-22)

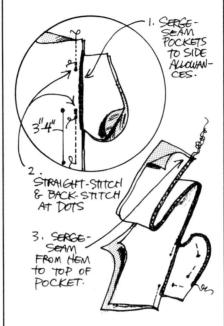

Fig. 9-22 Serge an easy inseam pocket in pants or skirts.

3. Beginning at the hemline, serge-seam up the side. When you reach the lower pocket edge, angle off the side seam onto the pocket, pulling the inside curve out straight in front of the foot as you serge over it. Then continue serging around the outer pocket edge.

4. Press the pockets toward the front and machine-baste them in place before finishing the waistline edge.

Top inseam pocket

When serging an inseam pocket in a jacket or coat or in a dress or jacket without a waistline seam, the previous technique will be changed slightly. For accuracy and to avoid cutting into the garment fabric with the knives, you must serge toward the pocket from both the top and bottom, overlapping the stitching on the outer pocket edge:

1. Serge-seam the pocket pieces to the side seam, right sides together, without trimming the edge.

2. Reinforce the pocket opening by straight-stitching and back-stitching at both ends for 3" to 4". (Fig. 9-23)

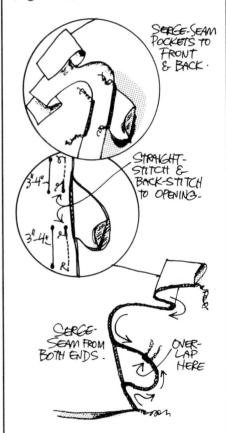

Fig. 9-23 Vary the seaming direction for inseam pockets in tops.

3. Serge-seam the underarm seam, right sides together, starting from the sleeve edge or armscye (depending on whether or not you have already applied the sleeves). End the seam on the outer pocket edge.

4. Complete the side seam by beginning at the lower hem edge, overlapping the other stitching on the pocket for about 1".

Front-hip pockets

Use your serger to construct this flattering pocket style in a jiffy:

1. Serge-seam the pocket facing to the front pocket edge right sides together, reinforcing the slanted or curved seamline using the technique on page 30. One of the easiest options is to fuse a strip of fusible interfacing to the edge and serge-seam over it. (Fig. 9-24)

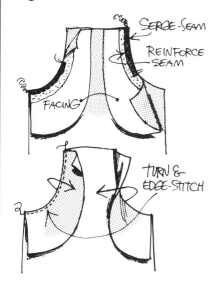

Fig. 9-24 Apply the facings first when making front-hip pockets.

2. Turn and press the facing to the inside and edge-stitch or under-stitch to hold it sharply in place.

3. Place the pockets right sides together with the facings and serge-seam around the outer pocket edges. (Fig. 9-25)

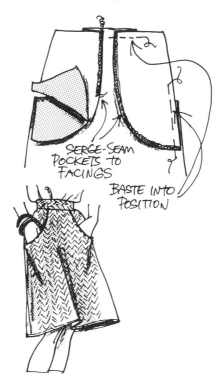

Fig. 9-25 Place the pockets right sides together with the facings and serge-seam the inner edges.

4. Machine-baste the pockets into position at the side and waistline seams before completing the garment.

Slash pocket

For a crisp, flat pocket opening anywhere on the garment, straight-stitch to create a rectangular opening:

1. Press a pinked rectangle of fusible interfacing to the underside of the fabric over the area where the opening will be cut. Mark the slash rectangle on the interfacing, with cutting lines angling to the corners. (Fig. 9-26)

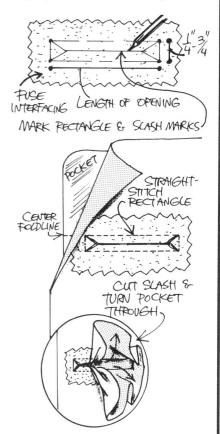

Fig. 9-26 Mark the slash opening on fusible interfacing as a foolproof guideline.

2. Cut a rectangle the width you will make the underpocket (at least 1" wider than the opening) and twice the pocket depth. Round all four corners evenly. Press the pocket with the short ends together to mark the center foldline. Position the right side of the pocket rectangle on the right side of the fabric, centering the foldline over the top side of the slash rectangle marked on the underside.

3. Straight-stitch around the rectangle through all layers, cut on the slash lines, and turn and press the pocket to the underside.

4. Reinforce the opening, if desired, by top-stitching across the lower edge with the slash open. Fold the back pocket section down. Then top-stitch across the top and sides. (Fig. 9-27)

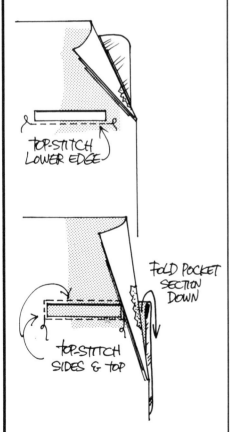

Fig. 9-27 Reinforce the slash by top-stitching all four edges. Pull through and knot the ends on the underside.

5. If you didn't top-stitch around the slash in step 4, fold the garment back to reveal the angled points. Straight-stitch through the points and the pocket to secure the ends of the opening. Then serge-seam the pocket edges. (Fig. 9-28)

Fig. 9-28 Serge-seam the sides and lower pocket edge to complete.

Self-welt pocket

Although it sounds difficult, this pocket technique takes only one more additional step than the slash-pocket method.

1. Complete the previous steps 1 through 3 beginning on page 105. Then refold the lower pocket section below the middle fold twice the distance of the opening. Press. Align the second fold with the top of the slash rectangle. (Fig. 9-29)

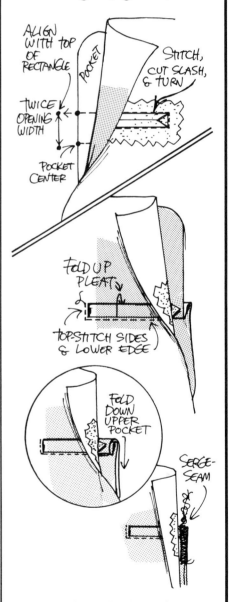

Fig. 9-29 Add a self-welt to a slash pocket by folding a pleat in the lower pocket section.

2. Fold a pleat in the lower pocket section equal to the width of the slash opening. Top-stitch from the right side around the sides and lower edge of the slash before the upper pocket section is turned down.

To add serged detailing, use a rolled-edge stitch to decoratively serge-finish the welt edge just after making the fold. Then continue constructing the pocket. (Fig. 9-30)

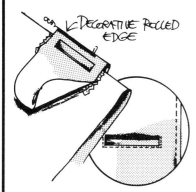

Fig. 9-30 Serge-finish the self-welt fold before top-stitching and serge-seaming the pocket edges.

3. Complete the opening following the previous step 5.

Inside patch pocket

For a sporty look, finish an opening anywhere on the garment and top-stitch a serge-finished patch pocket to the underside. Use this technique with a circular zipper opening (page 92) or any conventionally sewn slash.

1. Apply the zipper or other opening to the garment.

2. Cut lining or self fabric the size and shape of the desired pocket and serge-finish the edges.

3. Position the pocket piece under the opening and top-stitch in place from the right side using a straight-stitch, twin-needle, or decorative machine stitching. (Fig. 9-31)

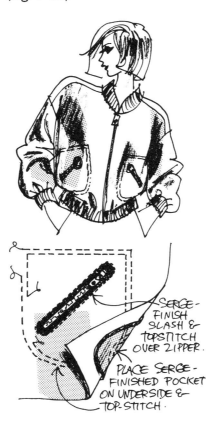

Fig. 9-31 Top-stitch a patch pocket to the underside after finishing the pocket opening.

For a simple slash opening on an inside patch pocket, use a facing rectangle for the slash. Cut it 1" larger than the slash opening on all sides. Apply it following the previous instructions for a slash pocket. After turning the rectangle to the wrong side, top-stitch around the slash to secure, then trim the excess facing fabric on the underside close to the stitching. Now top-stitch the pocket behind it, as discussed in the previous step 3. (Fig. 9-32)

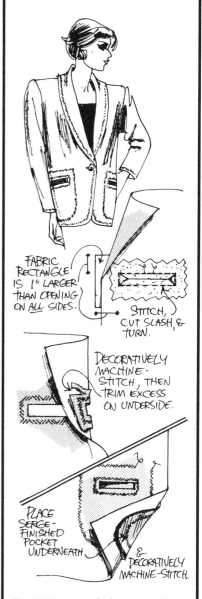

Fig. 9-32 Use a slash opening for an inside patch pocket.

NOTES

CHAPTER 10

SERGED HEMS

CHAPTER 10

Serged Hems

Hemming Options ✂ Slits ✂ Vents

Hemming Options

Professionally finish any hem on your garment by using serger techniques. (Fig. 10-1)

Choose the hem type depending on the weight of the fabric, the fabric weave (loosely woven or ravelly fabrics require a more durable finish), and the garment style. Hemming options range from simple serge-finished edges to serged-and-turned hems, enclosed edges, and serge-seaming a band or other trim to the edge.

Many neckline-finishing techniques (Chapter 4) and sleeve-finishing options (Chapter 5) can be used to finish hems. For example, ribbing or bias binding are often used for a matching finish on the neckline, cuff, and waistline edges of a simple top. (Fig. 10-2)

Fig. 10-1 Choose from a variety of serger

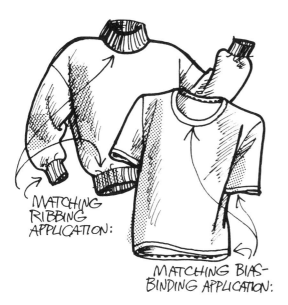

MATCHING RIBBING APPLICATION:

MATCHING BIAS-BINDING APPLICATION:

Fig. 10-2 Hem with coordinating neckline and sleeve techniques when the style dictates.

Most patterns give hemming instructions but the techniques are usually for conventional sewing-machine construction. However, it is easy to convert to serger applications outlined in this chapter to finish your garments.

With serger techniques, you can usually reduce the hem depth, depending on the garment shape. In general, the straighter the shape, the deeper the hem. To determine the hem depth, use the following guidelines.

Hemming Guidelines

Garment type	Hem depth
Straight or split skirts	2" to 3"
Jackets	1-1/2" to 2"
Pants, tops, and sleeves	1" to 1-1/2"
Flared, split, and full skirts	1/4" to 1"

Use a quick unstitched hem on pants or on sleeves with two seamlines. Cut hem allowances 2" for sleeves and 3" for pants. Serge-finish and press up the hem, then stitch-in-the-ditch of the seamlines vertically from the right side to hold it in place. (Fig. 10-3)

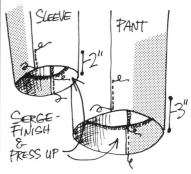

SLEEVE   PANT

2"

3"

SERGE-FINISH & PRESS UP

Fig. 10-3 Quickly hem a sleeve or pantleg by pressing up the allowance and stitching-in-the-ditch through the hem.

In most cases, complete the hem last, after finishing the other garment construction. Try on the garment for more accurate hem measurement. When making a fuller or bias-cut skirt, allow it to hang from the waistline for 24 hours before hemming so the fabric can stretch and settle before measuring.

Test hemming techniques on your fabric to determine the best hem allowance and finish. For example, a serge-finished hem may not be appropriate on a singleknit because the fabric will roll to the right side on the crosswise grain. Instead, a serged-and-turned hem (see Fig. 10-5) will provide the weight needed to prevent the fabric from rolling.

Serge-finished edges

For one of the easiest hem types, simply serge-finish the edge using one of several stitch options. Apply the serging on either a single layer or a fold. On any serge-finished edge, the stitching will be exposed on the right side of the garment. (Fig. 10-4)

When serge-finishing edges, keep these general guidelines in mind:

✄ Use a 2-, 3-, or 4-thread stitch to serge-finish a hem, depending on the weight of the fabric and your personal preference.

✄ Narrower serge-finished edges are more durable than wider ones.

✄ Serge-finishing is the most common hemming option for lightweight and delicate fabrics for which a serged-and-turned hem may be too bulky.

✄ If the serge-finished edge pulls away from a sheer or loosely woven fabric, use the serged-fold technique illustrated in Fig. 10-4.

Characteristics of a serged edge will vary with the length of the stitch and the type of thread used. Using a rolled edge, for example, a satin-length stitch with woolly nylon will give a firmer, heavier edge while a medium-length stitch using rayon thread will give a light-weight finish.

A serged edge-finish will be less obvious when using a lighter-weight thread and a longer stitch length. A 2-thread rolled edge using machine embroidery thread will create a fine delicately finished edge.

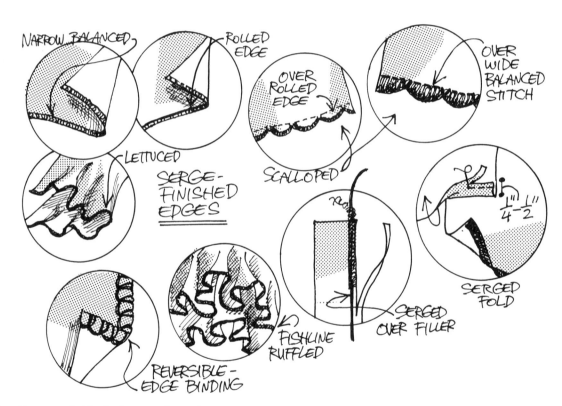

Fig. 10-4 Use serge-finished edges as a decorative accent.

Serge-finished Edges

Finish	Appropriate Fabrics	Page Reference	Uses	How-tos
Narrow balanced	Medium- to heavy-weights; when fabric will not roll	22	Hems, ruffles (for nonbulky finish)	Adjust for satin-length, narrow- to medium-width, balanced 3-thread stitch.
Rolled edge	Lightweight and sheer fabrics	23	Hems, ruffles	Adjust for short to mediumlength, 2- or 3-thread rolled edge.
Lettuced	Stretchy or bias fabrics	44	Hems, ruffles, collars	Stretch while serging a satin-length rolled edge. (Use a .7 differential-feed setting.)
Scalloped	Light- to medium-weights	112	Hems, ruffles, collars	Use a sewing machine blindhem (with tightened needle tension) over rolled or balanced edge.
Serged fold	Any	112	Stabilization when serging any of above stitches or a short, wide, balanced 3-thread stitch.	Turn 1/4" to 1/2" to wrong side and top-stitch close to fold. Trim close to top-stitching before serging over fold.
Serged over filler cord	Any	37	Hems, ruffles, front openings (for stabilization or a corded effect)	Serge over filler cord, selvage, stay tape, or elastic.
Fishline ruffled	Bias or stretchy crossgrain fabric	112	Hems, ruffles, collars	Serge a rolled edge over clear fishline using short- to medium-length stitch and filler-cord technique. (Stretch to flounce AFTER serging.)
Reversible-edge binding	Medium- to heavy-weights	112	Hems, collars	Adjust for short, narrow stitch with heavy thread in upper looper, loosen upper looper tension and tighten lower looper tension so thread wraps edge.

Serged-and-turned hems

Another quick hem-finish technique is to serge the edge, turn it to the underside, and top-stitch it in place. A wide range of options are available. (Fig. 10-5)

For a contrasting hem especially suitable on reversible fabrics, the edge can be decoratively serge-finished from the wrong side, then turned to the right side for top-stitching. (See Fig. 9-8)

Many turned hems are secured with conventional sewing-machine stitching, a quick and durable option repeatedly seen in ready-to-wear, giving the garment a sportier look. Because the top-stitching is visible on the right side of the garment, be sure it is an

When hemming an edge that will receive excessive stress or one designed to stretch during wear (such as on a knit top or a pushup sleeve), a good hemming choice is top-stitching with a stretchable twin-needle or zigzag stitch.

equal distance from the folded hem edge. Top-stitch using a straight-stitch, twin-needle, zigzag, or decorative sewing-machine stitch. (Fig. 10-6)

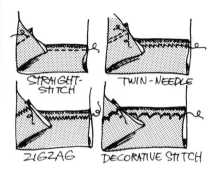

Fig. 10-6 Top-stitch a turned hem using your sewing machine.

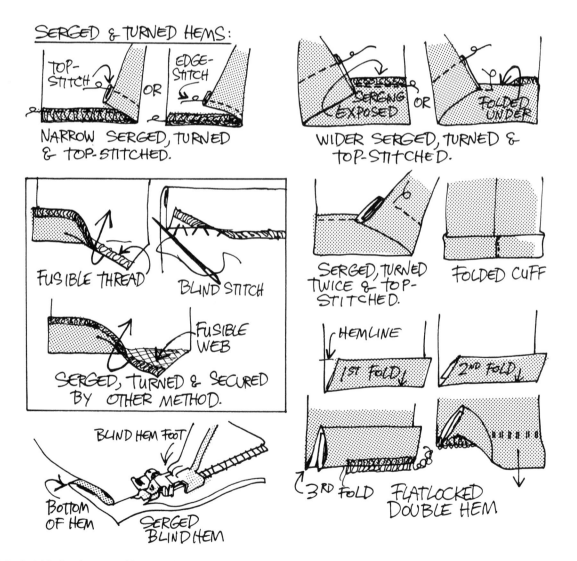

Fig. 10-5 Quickly finish a turned hem with serging.

Serged-and-Turned Hems

Finish	Appropriate Fabrics	Page Reference	Uses	How-tos
Narrow serged, turned, and top-stitched	Any; especially good for silky and knit fabric	114	Full skirt hems, ruffles, shirttail hems, necklines	Serge-finish using wide medium-length, balanced 3-thread stitch. Turn width of serging to wrong side and top-stitch.
Wider serged, turned, and topstitched	Any; good for medium- to heavy-weights	114	Hems on straight skirts, sleeves, jackets, pants	Serge-finish as above. Turn hem allowance to wrong side. Top-stitch next to serging or turn stitching under before top-stitching.
Serged, turned, and secured by other method	Any	114	Any	• Serge-finish as above using fusible thread in lower looper; turn and fuse. • Serge-finish as above over strip of fusible web; turn and fuse. • Serge-finish as above; turn and hand-stitch.
Serged, turned twice, and topstitched	Any; especially good for sheer and lightweight fabric	114	Full skirt hems, ruffles, shirttail hems	Serge-finish as above; turn width of serged stitch twice, and top-stitch.
Folded cuff	Medium- to heavyweights	61	Pants, sleeves	Serge-finish and fold up deep hem. Turn up cuff and secure at seamlines.
Serged blindhem	Sweatshirting, spongy knits	114	Wider hems	Fold as for conventional blindhem. Serge over fold using long, wide, balanced 3-thread stitch, catching needle thread only in fold. For accuracy, use serger blindhem foot.
Flatlocked double hem	Sweatshirting, medium-weights	114	Hems on sportswear and activewear	Fold half hem allowance twice to wrong side then fold again to right side. Flatlock on last fold using long, wide, 2- or 3-thread flatlock, catching needle just inside fold.

Top-stitch again close to the folded hem edge for a more durable finish. The row of stitching creases the edge permanently on a stubborn knit and gives a sporty look to any hem. (Fig. 10-7)

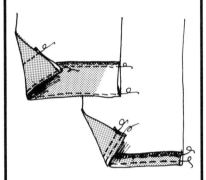

Fig. 10-7 Use a second row of top-stitching for a crisp, sporty hem.

When finishing a curved edge, serge-finish the raw edge, using a 1.5 or 2.0 differential-feed setting to ease in the fullness on inside curves and a .7 setting to stretch the edge on outside curves. This technique works especially well on curved shirttail hems. (If your serger does not have differential feed, manually ease-plus on inside curves, following the instructions in Fig. 3-6, and stretch gently in front of and behind the presser foot on outside curves.) For more stubborn curved hems, use the other serge-gathering techniques beginning on page 66.

Serge-finish the edges of a knit jersey garment to stabilize them and prevent rolling. The serging needleline is also a handy guideline for turning the edge (either once for a simple serged-and-turned hem or twice for a double-fold hem) before top-stitching.

When serging a blindhem, the serger stitches will be more obvious than those of a conventional sewing-machine blindhem.

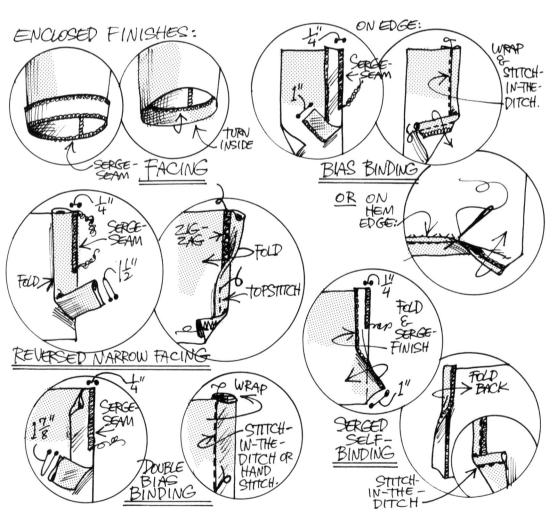

Fig. 10-8 Enclose the edge with a binding or facing.

Enclosed finishes

Try a number of speedy serger techniques to neatly enclose the hem (either on the edge or after the hem is turned) and stabilize it at the same time. Choose from self-fabric, matching fabric, or a contrasting fabric for any of the enclosure techniques. (Fig. 10-8)

A hem facing usually is usually applied to a curved or shaped edge. Cut the facing from lighter-weight fabric when you want to reduce the bulk of finishing a heavier fabric hem.

> When applying bias binding to any edge (see Fig. 10-8), the binding strip width can vary depending on the width of the seam used to apply it and the bulk of the seam allowance it must be wrapped over. Always test first and alter the strip width if necessary. If you prefer a binding over a seam allowance wider than the serged stitch width, straight-stitch the seam and serge-finish the allowances together so they can be wrapped easily. Calculate the binding width by adding the amount to be used in the seam allowance(s), the amount needed to wrap both sides of the binding, the amount turned under (if any), and the amount of the underside extension (usually 1/4") to catch the top-stitching.

Enclosed Finishes

Finish	Appropriate Fabrics	Page References	Uses	How-tos
Facing	Any	39	Lower and sleeve hems, front openings, necklines, pockets	Serge-seam facing to one side. Turn to other side for hemming.
Reversed narrow facing	Knits, light- to medium-weights	40	Necklines, hems, pockets	Serge-seam doubled facing to wrong side. Zigzag allowance to garment. Fold facing to right side and top-stitch.
Bias binding	Any; especially good for heavier or loosely woven	45	Hems, pockets, plackets, necklines	Serge-seam binding strip to garment or hem edge, right sides together. Wrap to wrong side and straight-stitch or hand-stitch.
Double-bias binding	Light- to medium-weights	115	Hems, pockets, plackets, necklines	Apply binding as above, using a doubled binding strip.
Serged self-binding	Any	38	Straight edges of wovens, any edges on knits	Serge-finish edge. Press to right side and serge over fold. Wrap to wrong side and stitch-in-the-ditch.

Consider these enclosed-finish variations:

✄ When a single-layer strip or facing is used to enclose the edge, choose from three finishing options for the binding or facing: 1) straight-stitch a serge-finished edge to the underside; 2) turn the serge-finishing under and straight-stitch for a clean finish; or 3) straight-stitch an unfinished edge and trim close to the stitching (for a quick finish for knits, bias, or nonravelly fabrics). (Fig. 10-9)

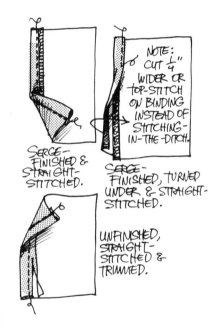

Fig. 10-9 Decide how to finish the binding or facing edge before applying it.

✄ Alter the bias-binding finish on any wider hem by using a wide matching or contrasting bias strip of any lightweight fabric. The wider binding both neatly finishes the edge and interfaces the hem, providing body, support, and a softer creaseline.

Follow these steps:

1. Measure the hem an even depth and press up lightly. Ease out any fullness, using one of the serge-gathering techniques beginning on page 66.

2. Cut a bias strip 1-1/4" wider than the finished hem depth. If piecing is necessary, serge the strip ends together on the straight of grain.

3. With the binding and the hem edge right sides together, serge-seam using a wide, balanced stitch. If necessary, minimize stretching by using the differential feed (or ease-plus) while serging. (Fig. 10-10)

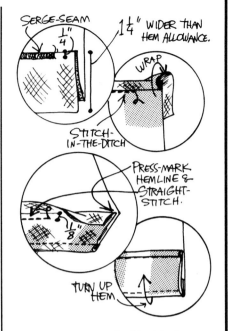

Fig. 10-10 Use a wider bias binding on the hem edge to interface a turned-up hem.

4. Wrap the binding around the seam allowances to the wrong side (to act as an interfacing) and stitch-in-the-ditch of the seamline. Press-mark the hem and the interfacing, folding the interfacing back on itself (for a soft crease at the hemline).

5. Straight-stitch the interfacing to the hem allowance 1/8" from the pressed fold. Hem by hand-stitching inside the upper hem edge.

Serged bands and trims

Serge-seam ruffles, lace, ribbing, or other trim to a garment edge as a simple hemming technique. The band or trim provides an attractive decorative treatment and also stabilizes the cut edge. (Fig. 10-11)

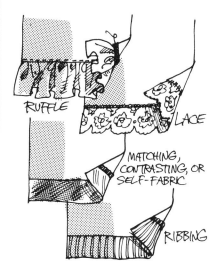

Fig. 10-11 Hem a garment by serge-seaming a band or trim to the edge.

Apply ruffles according to the directions on page 72. Flatlock flat lace to a garment hem with either right or wrong sides together. Before flatlocking, serge-finish the garment edges for added durability. When applying serged bands and trims, consider cutting them out of self-, matching, or contrasting fabric.

Ribbing is one of the most common trims used as a hem finish. Cut ribbed bands in various widths and lengths depending on the design of the garment and where they will be used.

When ribbing is not available, substitute knit self-fabric. This fabric will probably have less stretch than ribbing, so cut the band proportionately longer.

Follow these general ribbing pointers:

✄ The more a ribbing band is stretched during application, the more it will "cup" to the body. To apply ribbing at the lower edge of a waist-length garment, cut the ribbing 2/3 the length of the garment opening. For a hip-length or longer application, cut the band at least 3/4 the length of the garment's lower edge. Apply the ribbing following directions for a ribbed cuff on page 60.

✄ When a ribbing band is applied to a straight edge (such as a front opening or the top of a pocket), cut the ribbing the same length as the garment edge. Do not stretch while applying.

✄ Because of ribbing's variance in stretch and recovery, fit a ribbing strip (folded lengthwise) around the body to find the desired length before cutting.

Slits

Any loose hem edge can include a slit. (On speedy serged garments, eliminate slits unless they add an important design element or are used for fitting or walking ease.) You can quickly serge a simple slit in casual garments or serge-finish a constructed slit in a more tailored style.

Quick hem slit

This simple slit is completely faced by the hem allowance:

1. Before construction, trim the slit seam allowances to 1/4".

2. Serge-seam to the top of the slit, stopping with the needle in the fabric. Raise the presser foot, pull the fabric behind the needle, lower the foot, and serge off the fabric edge. (Fig. 10-12)

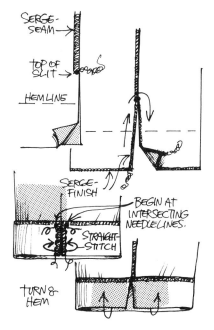

Fig. 10-12 Serge a simple slit using the hem allowance as a facing.

3. Serge-finish the hem edge and continuously serge-finish the slit edges without trimming.

4. With right sides together, fold up the hem allowance, matching the serge-finished slit edges. Beginning at the intersection of the serge-finishing needlelines, straight-stitch next to the vertical needlelines on both sides of the slit, back-stitching at both ends.

5. Turn the hem right side out and press carefully. Top-stitch the hem in place.

Easy serged slit

Choose this slit option for garments with 5/8" seam allowances which form a self-facing for the slit:

1. Serge-seam to the top of the slit with the needle on the seamline. Then pull the trimmed allowances out straight in front of the foot (as when serging an inside corner) and serge off the edge. (Fig. 10-13)

2. Serge-finish the hem edge and continuously serge-finish the slit edge without trimming. Press up the hem allowance to mark it.

3. With right sides together, fold up the hem allowance on the pressed line and straight-stitch on the 5/8" seam allowance at both sides of the slit.

4. Turn the hem to the underside. Continuously top-stitch the hem and around the slit, bar-tacking at the upper slit edge for reinforcement.

Serge-finished slit

Serge-finish and press open the edges of a wider slit, often found on a straight skirt pattern:

1. Separately serge-finish the hem and slit seam allowances, trimming off the upper slit corners. (Fig. 10-14)

2. Straight-stitch the seam to the top of the slit. Press open the seam and slit allowances.

3. Fold the slit allowances to the right side of the garment on the slit foldlines. Straight-stitch across the slit allowances on the garment hemline. Trim out the hem allowance in the slit to 1/4" from the stitching. (Or use the mitering technique shown on page 22.)

4. Turn the slit and hem to the underside and press carefully. Hand-stitch the hem in place.

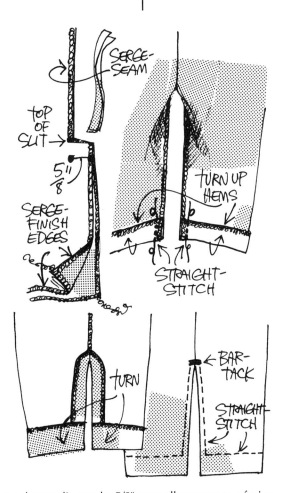

Fig. 10-13 For a deeper slit, use the 5/8" seam allowances as a facing.

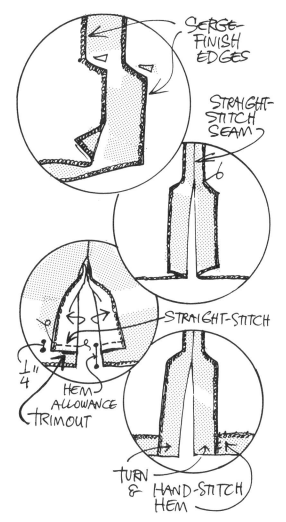

Fig. 10-14 When a slit facing is cut as part of the pattern, serge-finish all the edges.

Vents

On well-made jackets and skirts, you'll often find vents on sleeves and lower hems. A vent is similar to a slit but has an underlap, which is preferable for a tailored design.

1. Separately serge-finish the hem and vent seam allowances.

2. Straight-stitch the garment seam to the top of the vent and press the allowances open. (Fig. 10-15)

3. Clip to the dot on the left seam allowance to form the underlap.

4. Fold the serge-finished length-wise edge of the underlap to the wrong side and edge-stitch.

5. Press the underlap over the other vent allowance and top-stitch through all layers from the dot to the underlap edge, back-stitching at the ends.

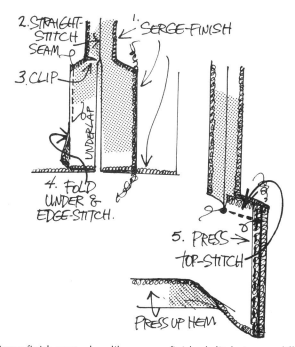

Fig. 10-15 Serge-finish vent edges like a serge-finished slit, but use a different construction technique.

For a pleated vent, don't serge-finish the lengthwise vent edges first. Clip and fold the underlap and serge-seam the lengthwise edges. Wrap the lengthwise seam allowance toward the vent and top-stitch at the top of the vent. Then fold up and hand-stitch the hem continuously. (Fig. 10-16)

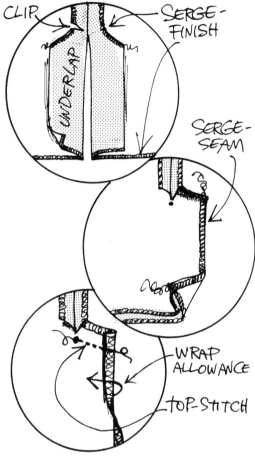

Fig. 10-16 Vary the vent technique to create a pleat out of the underlap.

6. Press up the hem. Finish the folded vent edge using one of the following options:

✂ On a lightweight fabric, fold out the vent and hand-stitch or top-stitch the hem where the vent allowance will be turned back over it. (Fig. 10-17)

✂ For a heavier fabric, fold out the vent and trim away the hem allowance on the underside of the vent seam allowance from 1/4" above the hemline to the vent foldline.

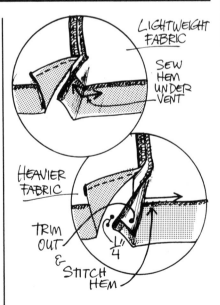

Fig. 10-17 Finish the vent before hemming the garment.

✂ Miter the vent corner (the most tailored and professional finish):

a. Press the hem and vent into the finished position, press-marking the corner point. Using a disappearing marker, mark the points where the hem edge meets the vent edge. (Fig. 10-18)

b. Open out the corner and draw a foldline from the corner through the corner-point marking and a stitching line between the two points where the edges met.

c. Fold on the foldline and match the edge markings on the stitching line. Serge-seam on the stitching line, turn, and press the corner to a sharp point.

7. Hem the garment after folding and pressing the vent into position. For most tailored garments with a vent, blind-stitch the hem by hand. For a sportier finish, top-stitch the hem from the right side.

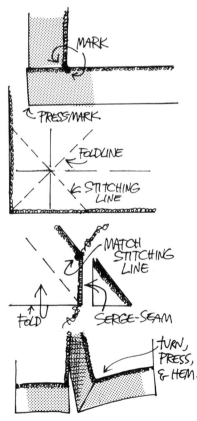

Fig. 10-18 Easily miter the vent corners, if you prefer.

CHAPTER 11

FINISHING TOUCHES

Finishing Touches

Shoulder Pads ✄ Belt Loops ✄ Bows ✄ Rosettes ✄ Spaghetti Straps ✄ Sleeve Headers

By now you should know the best serger techniques for constructing garments, but it's often the extra details that will turn your creation into a professional-looking masterpiece. Use your serger to add finishing touches, too.

Shoulder Pads

Shoulder pads can be an important factor in the fit of your garment. Check your pattern instructions to determine whether the style was designed for shoulder pads (the shoulder line and sleeve cap will be shaped to accommodate them). Then determine the style and size of shoulder pad you prefer by trying on several different sets as you construct the garment. (Fig. 11-1)

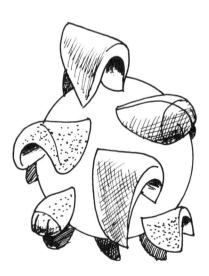

Fig. 11-1 Select a style and size of shoulder pad to best suit the garment.

For easy removal when washing and drycleaning, attach shoulder pads using *Velcro* strips on the shoulder seamline. With this attachment method, the shoulder pads can also be transferred to other garments. Sew the soft side of the *Velcro* to the shoulder seam and the hooked side to the shoulder pad. (See page 30 for the fastest application techniques while reinforcing the shoulder seams.)

Cover the shoulder pads in unlined garments. Although shoulder pads can be purchased already covered, you can easily cover less expensive ones using your serger. Follow these tips when selecting covering fabric:

✄ Use a smooth, lightweight woven or knit fabric—self-fabric, lining, or matching fabric are all options.

✄ Match the fabric to the garment color, if possible. Or cover the pads using a basic color (black for dark-colored garments and white or nude for light-colored ones).

> Create a handy shoulder pad wardrobe. Select tricot fabric or fusible interfacing in nude, white, and black. Cover one or two pair in each color. Tricot works well because it molds nicely to the pads. The advantage of interfacing is that it can be fused to the pads after covering them.

To cover a shoulder pad, cut a fabric square large enough to cover the pad with a 1/2" allowance.

1. Place the pad diagonally on the wrong side of the square. (Fig. 11-2)

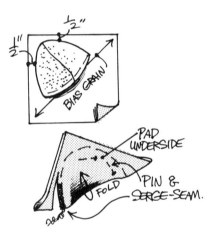

Fig. 11-2 Quickly cover a shoulder pad by serge-seaming through the outer edge of the pad sandwiched in covering fabric.

2. Fold the fabric over the pad, smoothing out the fullness. On both the top and underside, pin in the center of the pad to secure the fabric.

When you'll be attaching a shoulder pad with *Velcro*, mark the strip placement on the topside of the cover after folding the fabric. Remove the cover, straight-stitch the *Velcro* to it, then refold and pin the cover over the pad. (Fig. 11-3)

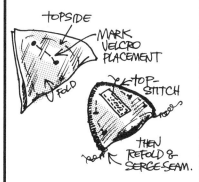

Fig. 11-3 For easy shoulder pad attachment, top-stitch *Velcro* to the cover before serge-seaming.

3. From the underside, serge-seam the raw edges using a wide, balanced stitch and catching the pad edge in the stitching.

If the shoulder pad is too wide and will show at the neckline, serge off any excess while seaming the edges. (Fig. 11-4)

Fig. 11-4 Reduce a shoulder pad by trimming off any excess while serge-seaming.

Belt Loops

Belt loops are not only functional, but also add fashion detail to a garment.

Fabric loops

Quickly serge belt loops continuously by cutting and finishing one long fabric strip. Determine the strip length by adding 3/4" to the width of your belt and multiplying by the number of loops needed (usually five). The strip width will vary with the serging technique (Fig. 11-5):

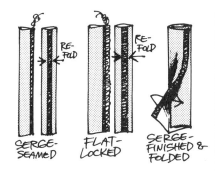

Fig. 11-5 Make belt loops by serge-finishing a long strip using one of three methods.

Serge-seamed—Cut the loop strip twice the finished width plus 1/2" for seam allowances. Fold it wrong sides together and serge-seam the long edges. Refold so the seam is centered on the underside of the strip.

Flatlocked—Cut the strip twice the finished loop width. With wrong sides together, flatlock the long edges together, allowing the stitches to hang halfway off the fabric. Pull the seam flat (by inserting small scissors or a knitting needle inside the strip) and refold as for the serge-seamed method.

Serge-finished and folded— Cut the loop strip three times the finished width. Serge-finish one long edge. Fold into thirds lengthwise with wrong sides together.

After finishing the strip, edge-stitch or decoratively serge-finish both sides. Cut the strip into loop sections and serge-finish all ends. Apply the loops by folding the ends under and top-stitching them to the garment. (Fig. 11-6)

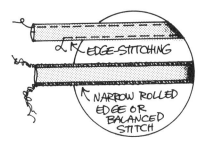

Fig. 11-6 Flatten the loops by stitching over the long edges of the strip before cutting.

Quickly prevent fraying of the loop ends by marking the cutting lines on the finished strip and dabbing them with seam sealant. After it dries, cut the strip into the loop sections and apply without serge-finishing.

Thread-chain loops

Use serger thread chain to make less conspicuous belt loops. Adjust your serger for a satin-length rolled edge or narrow balanced stitch and simply serge off a long thread chain. For more durable loops, serge over several strands of matching filler cord (such as buttonhole twist or crochet thread), following the instructions on page 37.

> **Keep extra thread chain handy to save valuable time when finishing a garment. After doing any serging using the previous settings, serge off several extra yards of thread chain. Store your supply in a large plastic baggie for fast selection.**

Using a large-eyed needle, draw the thread chain ends through the garment to the wrong side. Knot both ends securely and dab them with seam sealant to secure. For more durability, knot the ends together on the underside. (Fig. 11-7)

> **Also use thread chain for the eye of a hook and eye or to anchor a lining to a hem, sewing one end of the chain to the garment hem and the other to the lining hem, allowing 1" to 2" for ease. (Fig. 11-8)**

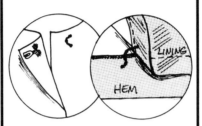

Fig. 11-8 Use thread chain for other finishing touches.

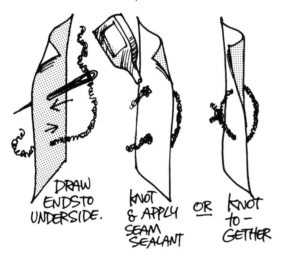

Fig. 11-7 Make simple thread-chain belt loops to match the garment.

Bows

Easily serge fabric bows of all sizes, shapes, and descriptions without the extra seam trimming required when using traditional construction methods.

Quick-serged bows

Create beautiful bows, using serge-finishing techniques. Apply a satin-length rolled edge to either a single layer or two layers placed wrong sides together. Two thread colors or two contrasting fabrics will create a unique effect. For the simplest bow, decoratively serge-finish the edges of a long strip and knot it into a bow. (Fig. 11-9)

Fig. 11-9 Fashion the speediest bow by serge-finishing and knotting a long fabric strip.

Make another speedy bow variation by wrapping a serged tie around the center of a serged bow.

Tie construction:

Clean-finished tie—For width, cut a strip two times the width of the finished tie plus 1/2". For length, cut it twice the amount of the center of the bow plus 1/2". Fold the strip in half lengthwise with wrong sides together and serge-seam. Refold, centering the seam, and serge-finish the ends. (Fig. 11-10)

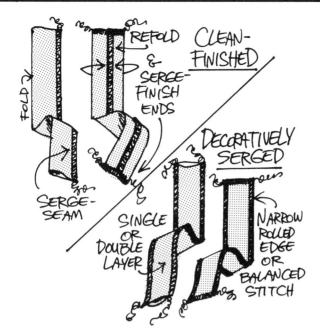

Fig. 11-10 Serge a tie to wrap around the center of the bow.

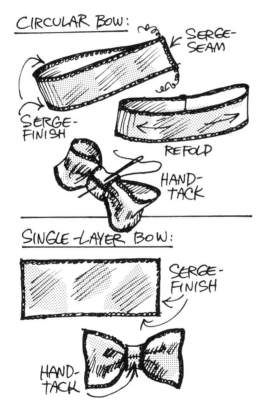

Fig. 11-11 Quickly make serge-finished bows—either circular or single-layer.

Decoratively serged tie—Cut a strip the width of the tie (or cut a double width and fold it in half, wrong sides together). Decoratively serge-finish all four edges.

Bow construction:

Circular bow:

1. Cut a fabric strip twice the finished bow length and serge-finish both long edges.

2. With wrong sides together, serge-seam the ends into a circle.

3. Refold, centering the seam on the underside.

4. Wrap the tie around the center of the bow and hand-stitch. (Fig. 11-11)

Single-layer bow—For heavier or crisper fabric, cut a rectangle or square of fabric the size of the finished bow. Decoratively serge-finish all four edges, wrap the tie tightly around the center, and hand-stitch.

> For an interesting bow shape, serge-finish a circle or an oval to make a single-layer bow. To make a lettuced bow, cut the fabric on the bias and lettuce the edge by stretching while serge-finishing . (Fig. 11-12)

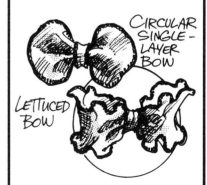

Fig. 11-12 Design novelty bows by changing the shape or edge-finish.

Interfaced bow

Interface a larger bow with crinoline for a shape-retaining, bouffant effect:

1. Cut out the fabric and crinoline as shown in Fig. 11-13, including a 7" by 4" fabric rectangle for the tie.

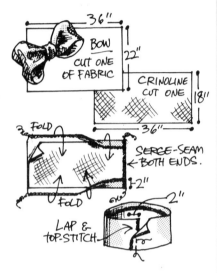

Fig. 11-13 Create a large, clean-finished, interfaced bow.

2. Serge-finish the long edges of the bow.

3. Center the crinoline on the wrong side of the bow. Press 2" of each long edge to the wrong side over the crinoline and serge-finish the bow ends.

4. Lap the ends, forming a circle, and top- or hand-stitch to secure.

5. Construct the tie using the previous clean-finished method, wrap it around the bow and hand-stitch.

Rosettes

Serge a rosette by folding or serge-finishing a long fabric strip, serge-gathering one edge, and shaping the altered strip like a flower. Chiffon, georgette, satin, lace, and lighter-weight knits are all good fabric choices.

✂ When possible, cut the fabric strip on the bias for the prettiest effect. Or cut it on the crosswise grain.

✂ Cut the strip 36" to 45" long by 1" to 2-1/2" wide. Or for the fullest rosette, cut the fabric double width and fold it in half lengthwise.

✂ Serge-finish the strip edges using one of the methods listed in the chart on page 113.

> **Make a ruffled rosette by using ribbing, interlock, or bias-cut chiffon, and lettucing one long edge.**

To make a rosette:

1. Decoratively serge-finish one long edge of the fabric strip or fold a double strip in half lengthwise and serge-finish the fold, if desired. (Fig. 11-14)

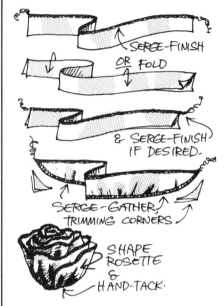

Fig. 11-14 Form rosettes from long strips of lightweight fabric.

2. Serge-gather (see page 66) the other long edge of the strip, tapering the ends.

3. Gather from one end, shaping the strip into a flower. Hand-tack the lower edges together and hand-stitch the rosette to the garment.

> **Serge-gather finished lace trim to make a pretty lace rosette. (Fig. 11-15)**
>
>
>
> Fig. 11-15 Scalloped-edge lace trim makes a fluffy rosette.

Spaghetti Straps

Follow a few simple steps to make quick and easy spaghetti straps using your serger. Cut the straps on the bias for smoother turning during construction and a softer, body-conforming finish. For ease in turning, make one strap at a time instead of a longer one that will be cut in two.

Thread-chain method

1. Cut a strip 1-1/4" wide for a narrow strap. For a wider strap, cut a strip twice the desired width plus 1/2".

2. Adjust for a short, narrow, balanced stitch or a rolled edge. Serge a thread chain several inches longer than the finished strap. Don't cut the chain.

3. Fold the strip right sides together around the thread chain and serge-seam the long cut edges, enclosing the chain. Keep the chain near the fold so that it isn't caught in the seaming. (Fig. 11-16)

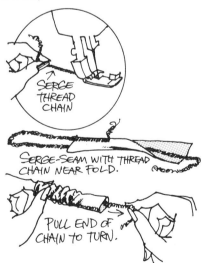

Fig. 11-16 Using a lightweight, silky fabric, construct a quick spaghetti strap.

4. Pull the thread chain gently to turn the strap right side out.

> **For the thread-chain technique, use lightweight, silky fabric, which will turn easily. When the spaghetti strap fabric is coarser, follow the loop-turner method below.**

Loop-turner method

Fold the fabric strip right sides together. Serge-seam and chain off for approximately 6" to 8". Insert a loop turner through the tube, catch the chain, and gently turn the strap right side out. (Fig. 11-17)

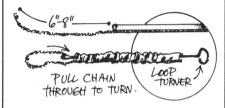

Fig. 11-17 When the fabric won't turn easily, use a loop turner to pull the thread chain through.

> **Make a narrow strap without turning by serge-seaming with wrong sides together. Then refold the strap, centering the seam on the underside. Keep a wider strap flat by decoratively serge-finishing or top-stitching both long edges. (Fig. 11-18)**

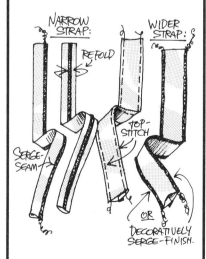

Fig. 11-18 To eliminate turning the strap, serge-seam with wrong sides together.

Sleeve Headers

Give shape to puffed sleeves by constructing serge-gathered sleeve headers in minutes:

1. Cut two 18" by 10" rectangles from crinoline or nylon net.

2. Fold the rectangles in half lengthwise. Serge-gather by tightening the needle tension (see page 66) or setting the differential feed at 1.5 to 2.0, rounding the corners. (Fig. 11-19)

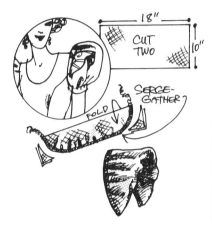

Fig. 11-19 Add sleeve headers to help shape puffed sleeves.

3. Adjust the serge-gathered edge to approximately 9" to 10", fitting it inside the sleeve over the top of shoulder.

4. Serge-seam the header to the sleeve seam, using a short stitch length to soften the cut edges and prevent irritation during wear.

Glossary

All-purpose or serger thread—All-purpose thread is usually cotton-covered polyester wound parallel on conventional spools. Standard serger thread has the same fiber content but is lighter in weight than all-purpose thread and is crosswound on cones or tubes so that it feeds easily during higher-speed serger sewing.

Balanced stitch—Serged stitching in which the upper- and lower-looper thread tensions are balanced so the threads meet at the edge of the fabric, forming loops.

Binding—A strip of fabric sewn to an edge, then wrapped around it and secured to hide the seam and the raw edge.

Chain off—To run the serger past the fabric edge, forming a thread chain. This will usually hold the stitching intact until the end is secured.

Clean-finish—Any technique in which the serging is hidden on the underside of the garment or on the inside of a section applied to the garment.

Clear the stitch finger—Remove the stitches which have formed over the serger's stitch finger. This is most often done by raising the presser foot and needle(s), pulling a little slack in the needle thread(s), and gently pulling the fabric toward the back of the machine.

Decorative—Any stitching on the outside of a garment or project that enhances design detail, usually using a decorative thread.

Decorative thread—Any thread other than all-purpose or serger thread, although even a contrasting color of these threads is technically considered decorative. Our favorite decorative serging threads include woolly nylon, rayon, pearl cotton, crochet thread, buttonhole twist, and metallic.

Ease-plus—A manual option to the differential feed, accomplished by force-feeding fabric under the front of the presser foot and holding it from exiting out the back.

Edge-stitch—A medium-length (10-12 stitches/inch) straight-stitch on a conventional sewing machine applied near the edge of the garment. Edge-stitching is often used to join two serge-finished layers.

Filler cord—Crochet thread, pearl cotton, buttonhole twist, or other heavy thread that simulates piping when serged over with a short, satin-length stitch.

Flatlock—A stitch type in which the needle thread is loose enough so the serged stitches flatten out on top of the fabric, forming decorative loops when the fabric is pulled apart. The underside will show a ladder effect of evenly spaced double parallel stitches. Use for both seaming and decorative stitching on a folded edge.

Heavy thread—Crochet thread, pearl cotton, or buttonhole twist used for serge-gathering or filler cord in serger piping.

Long stitch—A 4mm or 5mm serged stitch length.

Machine-baste—A long (6-8 stitches/inch) straight-stitch on a conventional sewing machine.

Matching thread—Thread the same color as (or that blends as well as possible with) the project fabric.

Medium-length stitch—A serged stitch length of about 3mm.

Medium-width stitch—A serged stitch width of about 3.5mm.

Narrow-width stitch—A 2mm to 3mm serged stitch width. Used to serge a narrow seam or edge.

Pin-fit the pattern—Pin the pattern pieces together on the seamlines and hold them up to your body to estimate the fit of the finished garment.

Ready-to-wear—Garments available for purchase through retail stores and mail-order outlets.

Rolled edge (finish or seam)—Also called a narrow rolled edge or hem, this stitch is created by altering the tension so that the raw edge rolls to the underside. A short stitch length creates an attractive satin-stitch edge.

Satin-stitch (satin-length)—A stitch length short enough to allow the thread used to cover the entire fabric over which it is serged. Appropriate for both a balanced stitch or a rolled edge.

Secure the thread chain—Using one of several possible methods to keep the ends of serged stitching from ravelling. Options include applying seam sealant and trimming the excess when dry, knotting the chain, feeding the chain under previous stitches using a hook or tapestry needle, or serging over previous stitches.

Serge-finish—Most often a medium-length, medium-width, balanced 3- or 3/4-thread stitch used to finish the edge of one layer during the construction process.

Serge-gather—Gathering an edged or fold by using of one of several serger techniques (see Chapter 6) before top-stitching or easing and serge-seaming it to the garment.

Serge-seam—Most often a wide, medium-length, balanced 3- or 3/4-thread stitch used to seam two layers together.

Short stitch—A .75mm to 2mm serged stitch length.

Stitch-in-the-ditch—Stitching directly on top of a previous seamline to secure another layer positioned on the underside. Often used for nearly invisible stitching when applying a binding to an edge.

Stitch types—Distinctive stitches formed by a serger (see page __). Most serger models feature a combination of stitch types. (Fig. ?)

Straight-stitch—A medium-length (10-12 stitches/inch) straight stitch on a conventional sewing machine.

Thread chain—The joined loops formed by serging on a properly threaded machine with no fabric.

Top-stitch—A conventional sewing-machine straight stitch (10-12 stitches/inch) used to attach one layer (often serge-finished) to another away from the garment edge. Top-stitching also can be used as a decorative design detail.

Wide stitch—A 5mm to 9mm serged stitch width.

Woolly nylon—One of our favorite decorative threads that became popular with the advent of serger sewing. A crimped nylon thread, it fluffs out to fill in any see-through spaces on a decorative edge.

Zigzag stitch—A basic sewing-machine stitch forming a series of short, sharp angles.

Mail-Order Resources

We recommend that every serger enthusiast develop a special relationship with his or her local dealers and retailers for convenient advice and inspiration, plus the ease of coordinating purchases. However, when specialty items cannot be found locally, or when a home-sewer lives several miles from a sewing retailer, mail-order specialists are a worthwhile option.

Authors' note:

In today's volatile business climate, any mail-order source list will change frequently. Please send your comments on any out-of-business notifications or unsatisfactory service to Tammy Young, 2269 Chestnut #269, San Francisco, CA 94123.

Key to Abbreviations and Symbols:

SASE = Self-addressed, stamped (first-class) envelope
L-SASE = Large SASE (2-oz. first-class postage)
 * = refundable with order
 # = for information, brochure, or catalog

Aardvark Adventures, P.O. Box 2449, Dept. TY, Livermore, CA 94551, 415/443-2687. Books, beads, buttons, bangles, plus an unusual assortment of related products. Decorative serging thread, including metallics. $2*#.

Clotilde, Inc., 1909 S.W. First Ave., Ft. Lauderdale, FL 33315, 800/772-2891. Wide range of supplies, including special serger threads and notions, other sewing tools and supplies, books, and videos. $1#.

The Cutting Edge, P.O. Box 397, St. Peters, MO 63376. Serger sewing patterns, acrylic serging yarn, shoulder pads, and miscellaneous serger notions. L-SASE#.

Madeira Marketing Ltd., 600 E. 9th St., Michigan City, IN 46360, 219/873-1000. Popular decorative threads. SASE#.

Mill End Store, Box 82098, Portland, OR 97282-0098, 503/786-1234. Broad selection of notions, trims, serger threads, and accessories. SASE#.

Nancy's Notions, Ltd., P.O. Box 683, Beaver Dam, WI 53916, 800/833-0690. Wide range of sewing notions and accessories, serger threads and tools, interfacings and fabrics, books, and videos. Free#.

National Thread & Supply, 695 Red Oak Rd., Stockbridge, GA 30281, 800/847-1001, ext. 1688; in GA, 404/389-9115. Name-brand sewing supplies and notions. Free#.

Newark Dressmaker Supply, P.O. Box 20730, Lehigh Valley, PA 18002-0730, 215/837-7500. Sewing notions, trims, buttons, decorative threads, and serger supplies. Free#.

Sew-Art International, P.O. Box 550, Bountiful, UT 84010. Decorative threads, notions, and accessories. Free#.

Sew/Fit Co., P.O. Box 565, La Grange, IL 60525, 800/547-4739. Sewing notions and accessories; modular tables for serger/sewing machine setup; books. Free#.

Sewing Emporium, 1079 Third Ave. #B, Chula Vista, CA 91910, 619/420-3490. Hard-to-find sewing notions, sewing machine and serger cabinets, machine accessories, and serger threads. $4*#.

The Sewing Place, 18770 Cox Ave., Saratoga, CA 95070. Sewing machine and serger needles and feet, plus books by Gale Grigg Hazen. Specify your brand and model when ordering machine accessories. L-SASE#.

Speed Stitch, 3113-D Broadpoint Dr., Harbor Heights, FL 33983, 800/874-4115. Machine-art kits and supplies, including all-purpose, decorative, and specialty serging threads, books, and accessories. $3*#.

Treadleart, 25834 Narbonne Ave., Lomita, CA 90717, 800/327-4222. Books, serging supplies, notions, decorative threads, and creative inspiration. $3#.

YLI Corporation, 482 N. Freedom Blvd., Provo, UT 84601, 800/854-1932 or 801/377-3900. Decorative, specialty, serger, and all-purpose threads, yarns, and ribbons. $2.50#.

Index

Adjustments, to pattern, 13-14
Banded cuff, 61
Banded necklines, 47
    band application, 47
    for V-neckline, 47-48
Banded pocket, 101-102
Banded sleeve placket, 57
Bands, serged, 118
Basting, 21
    pin, 4
Basting tape, 21
Belt loops
    fabric, 125
    thread-chain, 126
Binding, for sleeves, 62
Blouse, neckline finishes for, 52
Blouson effect, on ribbed sleeve, 60
Bound and lapped seam, 29
Bound necklines
    adding self-fabric/lace ruffle, 46
    binding application, 46
    guidelines for, 45
Bound seam, 27-28
Bound sleeve placket, 58
Bow(s)
    construction
        circular bow, 127
        single-layer bow, 127
    interfaced, 128
    quick-serged, 126-127
Buttonholes, stabilizing, 33
Buttonhole twist thread, 67
Chainstitched shirring, 70
Circular ribbing application, for
    round necklines, 43
Clean-finished cuff, 59-60
Closures
    elastic button loops, 93-94
    options for, 95
    zippers, 90-92
Collar application
    piped effect on collar edge, 51
    rounded collars, 51-52
    two-piece rectangular collars, 51
Combination gathering, 68
Combination seams
    bound, 27-28
    bound and lapped, 29
    enclosed serged, 27
    lapped, 28
    lapped-and-enclosed, 28
    serged flat-felled, 26
    serged French, 26-27
Construction basics
    basting, 21
    corners, 31
    curves, 32
    darts, 32
    interfacing techniques, 33

machine cleaning, 20
needle check and selection, 20
pinning, 21
pointers for serged seams, 29
reinforced seams, 30-31
seam types, 22-29
thread selection, 21
Construction order, 17-18
Construction secrets, 2
    cutting, 4
    gathering supplies, 3-4
    pin-basting, 4
    for pull-on pants, 7
    for pullover top, 5-6
    seaming, 5
    serger basics, 2
Construction techniques
    gathering, 66-69
    lining, 75-77
    for pleats, 74-75
    for ruffles, 72-73
    shirring, 70-71
    for tucks, 73-74
Corners
    inside, 31
    outside, 31
Cuffs
    banded, 61
    clean-finished, 59-60
    folded, 61
    quickest, 59
    ribbed, 60-61
        blouson effect, 60
Curves
    inside, 32
    outside, 32
Cutting, 4, 16
Darts, serging, 32
Decoratively self-bound neckline, 38-39
Decorative seams, 22
Differential-feed gathering, 66
Dolman sleeve, application of, 56
Doubled facing, for necklines, 40
Double pocket, with self-flap, 103
Drawstring, 87
Dress, lining, 75
Easy serged slit, 119
Easy-to-sew patterns, 10
Elastic
    gathering, 68
    measuring, 82
    pointers on, 80, 81
    selection guideline for, 81
    shirring, 70-71
    sport, 4, 84
    types of, 80, 81
Elastic button loops
    serge-covered cording, 94
    serged with clean-finished edge, 93

    serged with decorative stitching, 93
    serge over covered cording, 94
Elastic casing
    flounced, 63
    for sleeves, 62-63
Enclosed finishes, 115-117
    variations for, 117
Enclosed serged seam, 27
Fabric belt loops, 125
    flatlocked, 125
    serge-finished and folded, 125
    serge-seamed, 125
Fabric considerations, 11
    for banded placket, 57
    choosing fabric, 4
    for constructed waistbands, 86
    in cutting, 16
    in gathering, 66, 68
    in hemming, 114, 115, 116, 121
    for lining, 75
    and needles, 20
    pretreatment, 11-12
    in seaming, 21, 25
    for serge-finished edges, 112
    in serging, 17
Fabric selvage, neckline serged over, 37-38
Faced necklines
    doubled facing, 40
    reversed narrow facing, 40
    round neckline facing, 39-40
    V-neckline facing, 41
Facing
    doubled, 40
    eliminating, 11
    for keyhole openings, 48-49
    reversed narrow, 40
    for sleeves, 62
    V-neckline, 41
Filler cord, neckline serged over, 37
Filler-cord gathering, 68-69
    variations in, 69
Finger-pinning, 4
Finishes
    ribbed, 41-44
Finishing touches
    belt loops, 125-126
    bows, 126-128
    rosettes, 128
    shoulder pads, 124-125
    sleeve headers, 129
    spaghetti straps, 129
Fishline, ruffled edge, 112
Fitting, 12
    basting seams, 14
    making adjustments to pattern, 13-14
    measurements for, 12
    tips for, 12
Flat-felled seam, serged, 26
Flatlocked seam, 24

About the Authors

Naomi Baker is a nationally recognized serger sewing authority who writes regularly for major industry publications and has co-authored six previous Chilton books with Tammy Young. A home economics graduate of Iowa State University and former extension agent, she worked for Stretch & Sew for ten years. She specializes in technique research and development and is well known for her dressmaking skills.

Naomi has a sewing consulting business and appears across the country at special workshops and conventions. She lives and works in Springfield, Oregon, with her husband and family, huge fabric stash, and an enviable number of sergers and sewing machines.

Tammy Young is known for developing creative serger applications and for writing precise, detailed instructions. With a home economics degree from Oregon State University, she has an extensive background in the ready-to-wear fashion industry, as well as being a former extension agent and high school home economics teacher. Tammy has co-authored nine previous Chilton books.

Living and working in San Francisco's Marina District, Tammy founded and managed the *Sewing Update* and *Serger Update* newsletters before selling them in 1991. Now she enjoys working on creative projects and dreaming up ideas to try in her "spare time."

Other Books by the Authors

ABCs of Serging, Chilton Book Company, 1991, $16.95. The complete guide to serger sewing basics, by Tammy Young and Lori Bottom.

Distinctive Serger Gifts & Crafts, Chilton Book Company, 1989, $14.95. The first book with one-of-a-kind serger projects using ingenious methods and upscale ideas, by Naomi Baker and Tammy Young.

Innovative Serging, Chilton Book Company, 1989, $14.95. State-of-the-art techniques for overlock sewing, by Gail Brown and Tammy Young.

Innovative Sewing, Chilton Book Company, 1990, $14.95. The newest, best, and fastest sewing techniques, by Gail Brown and Tammy Young.

Know Your baby lock, Chilton Book Company, 1990, $16.95. Ornamental serging techniques for all baby lock serger models, by Naomi Baker and Tammy Young.

Know Your Pfaff Hobbylock, Chilton Book Company, 1991, $17.95. Ornamental serging techniques for all Hobbylock serger models, by Naomi Baker and Tammy Young.

Know Your Serger, Chilton Book Company, 1992, $16.95. Ornamental serging techniques and all-new projects for any serger brand, by Naomi Baker and Tammy Young.

Know Your White Superlock, Chilton Book Company, 1991, $16.95. Ornamental serging techniques for all Superlock serger models, by Naomi Baker and Tammy Young.

Simply Serge Any Fabric, Chilton Book Company, 1990, $14.95. Tips and techniques for successfully serging all types of fabric, by Naomi Baker and Tammy Young.

Taming Decorative Serging, by Tammy Young, self-published 1991, $14.95. A step-by-step workbook teaching special techniques for glamorous decorative serging.

Taming Your First Serger, by Lori Bottom, Tammy Young 1989, $14.95. A hands-on guide to basic serging skills in an easy-to-use workbook format.

Look for these titles in your local stores, or write for a complete, up-to-date listing: Tammy Young, 2269 Chestnut, Suite 269, San Francisco, CA 94123. To order, add $3.50 per book to the listed price for shipping and handling.